SCOTNOTES
Number 26

Sir David Lyndsay's

A Satire of the Three Estates

John Corbett

Association for Scottish Literary Studies 2009

Published by
Association for Scottish Literary Studies
Department of Scottish Literature
7 University Gardens
University of Glasgow
Glasgow G12 8QH
www.asls.org.uk

ASLS is a registered charity no. SC006535

First published 2009

Text © John Corbett

Illustrations © University of Glasgow
Reproduced by kind permission

A CIP catalogue for this title
is available from the British Library

ISBN 978-0-948877-95-7

The Association for Scottish Literary Studies
acknowledges the support of the Scottish Arts Council
towards the publication of this book

Printed by Bell & Bain Ltd, Glasgow

CONTENTS

		Page
1.	Introduction	1
2.	Sir David Lyndsay: his life and work	6
3.	The History of the Text	13
4.	*Dramatis Personae*	17
5.	A Summary of the Play	26
6.	Historical and Political Background	42
7.	Literary Influences on the Play	48
8.	Staging the Play in the 16th Century	54
9.	Language and Style	57
10.	Two Key Scenes	71
11.	Modern Versions and Productions	78
12.	The Influence of *Ane Satyre of the Thrie Estaitis*	82
13.	Conclusion	86
14.	Further Reading	84
15.	Timeline	90
16.	Vocabulary Answers	94

SCOTNOTES

Study guides to major Scottish writers and literary texts

Produced by the Education Committee
of the Association for Scottish Literary Studies

Series Editors
Lorna Borrowman Smith
Ronald Renton

Editorial Board
Ronald Renton, St Aloysius' College, Glasgow
(Convener, Education Committee, ASLS)
Jim Alison, HMI (retired)
Professor John Corbett, University of Glasgow
Dr Morna Fleming, Liberton High School
Professor Douglas Gifford, University of Glasgow
John Hodgart, Garnock Academy
Alan MacGillivray, Past President of ASLS
Catrina McGillivray, Newbattle Abbey College
Dr David Manderson, University of the West of Scotland
Dr Christopher Nicol, Galashiels Academy
Lorna Ramsay, Fairlie, Ayrshire
Professor Alan Riach, University of Glasgow
Dr Christine Robinson, Scottish Language Dictionaries
Dr Kenneth Simpson, University of Strathclyde
Lorna Borrowman Smith, formerly Wallace High School
Ailsa Stratton, Boroughmuir High School

THE ASSOCIATION FOR SCOTTISH LITERARY STUDIES aims to promote the study, teaching and writing of Scottish literature, and to further the study of the languages of Scotland.

To these ends, the ASLS publishes works of Scottish literature; literary criticism and in-depth reviews of Scottish books in Scottish Studies Review; short articles, features and news in ScotLit; and scholarly studies of language in Scottish Language. It also publishes New Writing Scotland, an annual anthology of new poetry, drama and short fiction, in Scots, English and Gaelic. ASLS has also prepared a range of teaching materials covering Scottish language and literature for use in schools.

All the above publications are available as a single 'package', in return for an annual subscription. Enquiries should be sent to:

ASLS, Department of Scottish Literature, 7 University Gardens, University of Glasgow, Glasgow G12 8QH. Tel/fax +44 (0)141 330 5309, e-mail **office@asls.org.uk** or visit our website at **www.asls.org.uk**

Notes and Acknowledgements

A Satire of the Three Estates is the modernised spelling of the title of Sir David Lyndsay's 16th century play. In Lyndsay's time there were several possible spellings of this title and of the names of the characters in the play, and even of the playwright's own name, which could be written 'Lyndsay', 'Lindesay', and so on. In this Scotnote, I use *Ane Satyre of the Thrie Estaitis* for the title of the play, 'Sir David Lyndsay' for its author, and one consistent early spelling for each of the characters' names. Other spellings are possible – which is well to remember of you are googling the play or its author. A further point to note is that in Older Scots the 'ne' in 'ane' was silent before a consonant like 's' in 'ane satyre'.

I have benefited from the encouragement and advice of the Education Committee of the Association for Scottish Literary Studies in the writing of this Scotnote. They have all been gude counsalls. Particular thanks must, however, go to Ronnie Renton who suggested the project to me, and to Duncan Jones, the ASLS general manager, without whom none of our bright ideas would reach your bookshelf. I would also like to acknowledge a longstanding debt of gratitude to Rod Lyall, whose teaching led me and many others towards an appreciation of older Scottish literature.

The illustrations are reproduced by kind permission of Glasgow University Library Special Collections Department. They show Flatterie; Veritie and Chastitie in the stocks; and Molly MacEwan's designs for the costumes of King Humanitie and Placebo, for the 1948 Edinburgh Festival production.

*Duncan Macrae as Flatterie in Tyrone Guthrie's
1948 production of* The Three Estates

Molly MacEwan's costume design for King Humanitie, for the 1948 production

Molly MacEwan's costume design for Placebo, for the 1948 production

Veritie (left) and Chastitie in the stocks, played by Ann Kristen and Edith MacArthur, in Tom Fleming's 1984–85 production.

1. INTRODUCTION

At the start of a long summer's day, in early June of the year 1552, in and around the town of Cupar in Fife, many of the folk woke up with a sense of excitement and anticipation. Some days before, a small group of players had appeared in the town. They had acted out some rude and comical sketches, and then one of the actors had proclaimed that on the 7th June, they would return with their troupe and perform a full play for the townsfolk. So far as we know, the performance on that summer's day, Whitsun Tuesday, was the first public outing of the full version of Sir David Lyndsay of the Mount's *Ane Satyre of the Thrie Estaitis*. The people who gathered on Castle Hill in Cupar to watch the performance, which started at seven in the morning and probably stretched over much of the day, would have seen something astonishing. A young Scottish king would be seduced, and his kingdom neglected. Flatterers and tricksters would run riot, taking advantage of the king's distraction to infiltrate the highest offices of the church, and bankrupt and oppress the common people. Two beautiful women, representing the virtues of truth and chastity, would be imprisoned in stocks, while a good and honest adviser would be prevented from gaining an audience with the king. However, just as the kingdom seemed to be descending into chaos, a character called Divyne Correctioun, a representative of God Himself would miraculously appear in the land, releasing the virtues of truth and chastity, and rekindling in the young king a sense of moral duty. Divyne Correctioun and the king would then call a parliament of the Three Estates – the three governing classes of churchmen, nobles and merchants – to reform Scotland's laws in favour of the common people.

At this point the play would be only half complete. After a comic interlude, the audience in Cupar, mostly common people themselves, would be treated to the grand theatrical spectacle of a mock parliamentary session, with the Three Estates walking backwards on their arrival to demonstrate their contempt for both Divyne Correctioun and the king. The session would be further disrupted by the arrival of John the Common-weill, the representative of ordinary folk. No doubt to cries of encouragement from the crowds, he would complain about the injustices that he and another typical poor man had suffered, mainly at the hands of greedy, vicious and largely uneducated churchmen. These churchmen would accuse John of heresy and threaten him with the stake. However, Divyne Correctioun would uphold John's complaint and demand that the Three Estates change their ways and vow to protect the common people of Scotland. The vices who had corrupted the king and exploited the people would be banished or publicly hanged, and a whole raft of specific legal measures would be announced, to ensure that churchmen had the education and the spiritual qualities necessary to care for their congregations. However, the conclusion of the play would be marked by the entrance of Folly, an ambiguous figure, whose antics would remind the audience that human nature is naturally inclined towards foolishness and corruption; more frightening still, he would also prophesy an imminent war against France. The play ends with the Herald who opened the proceedings blessing the audience, before exiting for a well-earned drink.

The play was performed in the open air, before an audience that would have included members of the nobility, churchmen, merchants and local craftsmen and their wives – a social mixture that mirrored the ranks of society seen in the play. The performing area would have been marked out, perhaps bordered by a ditch, and seating would have been set up to represent the king's throne and the parliamentary seats of the Three Estates. While some cast members performed their scenes, others remained seated watching them. Some of the players appeared through the audience, and, as sometimes happens in stage productions now, members of the audience might well have thought that the play was being interrupted by one of themselves: an angry commoner, a distracted poor man or even a fleeing thief. Some of the audience would have stayed with the play for its entire duration, which has been variously estimated as between four and nine hours. Other audience members would have strayed and returned, perhaps with a drink of ale; still others would have left early or arrived late.

The form of the play, therefore, reflects the way in which the first audience would have experienced it. *Ane Satyre of the Thrie Estaitis* is a series of episodes, linked by a strong, conventional, overarching theme. The individual fall from grace and eventual redemption of a young king is seen in relation to the general decline into corruption and then reformation of the state that he governs. Comic scenes illustrate the chaos that ensues when the ruler of a kingdom is seduced by worldly pleasures. The characters are easily-recognised moral or social stereotypes, many of them representative vices or virtues, while others are typical spokesmen for the lords, merchants, churchmen, or common folk. Minor characters are identified by their occupation (e.g. 'Taylour', tailor), their social position (e.g. 'Taylour's wife'), or their lack of either (e.g. the 'Pauper', a poor man). Several scenes in the play draw upon types of public performance that were not in themselves theatrical, but which similarly depended on spectacle and performance: religious sermons; the rituals of parliamentary sessions, including processions, debates and the proclamation of new laws; a public trial and even some hangings.

At the time of the play's first full performance, Cupar was the main town in the county of Fife and, since the end of the 13th century, it had been one of several places where Scottish kings had gathered together the parliament of the Three Estates, to make new laws. The town lay in the diocese of the cathedral of St Andrews, which was the religious centre of 16th century Scotland. The Cupar townsfolk would therefore have recognised the characters in the play immediately, and so those who arrived late or left early and thus saw only parts of the play would have enjoyed those episodes as reasonably self-contained segments. However, those who stayed the course of the day would have experienced a full, satisfying narrative that follows an arc from youthful innocence and social harmony through corrupt experience and social chaos, to a finale marked by personal redemption and social reformation – and a coda comprising a fool's satirical sting in the tail.

The play is written in the language of sixteenth century Scotland, a period characterised by the vivid use of spoken and written Scots by the highest and lowest classes in the land. The dramatic language of *Ane Satyre of the Thrie Estaitis* is by turns obscene and ceremonial, funny and formal, showing the playwright's confident command of a rich repertoire of dramatically appropriate verse forms. As with satire today, while some of the audience might simply have laughed at the many illustrations of human folly on display, others might have been shocked at the irreverent treatment of the upper classes and the church, and at the dramatic articulation of what its author saw as the cause of the many moral and political abuses of its time. *Ane Satyre of the Thrie Estaitis* reaches back to the medieval tradition of morality plays that staged the eternal conflict between good and evil, as represented by virtues and vices. But it also contains a mixture of broad, farcical entertainment spiced with sharp social criticism that characterises many of the most successful plays and television dramas today. It draws on further traditions, including French farces and *sotties,* which were popular comedies in which Folly is shown to be the vice that ultimately governs human behaviour. Lyndsay's play fashions something new from a range of earlier dramatic genres, and in doing so it becomes the source from which all subsequent Scottish theatrical performances spring.

This Scotnote serves as a concise introduction to the earliest surviving complete play-text in Scottish drama. I am fortunate in having been able to draw on a wealth of earlier editorial and critical scholarship to give a portrait of the play's accomplished author, sketch out the complicated history of the text itself, outline the characters and the plot, and place them in a historical and political context. Even the earliest surviving Scottish play did not suddenly spring from a void, and so we consider the possible influences on *Ane Satyre of the Thrie Estaitis,* and give an appreciation of the pungent and grand dramatic language in which the play is composed. Attention is drawn to some key scenes that will repay consideration by pupils, teachers and students; and the play's afterlife is briefly considered in sections that deal with modern productions of the medieval play, as well as several recent plays that share their illustrious predecessor's episodic, rambling nature and keen political intent.

A Satire of the Three Estates

Throughout the Scotnote, activities like the one below are suggested to engage your active interest, and so enhance your understanding and appreciation of *Ane Satyre of the Thrie Estaitis*. The readership of this Scotnote is likely to be a mixed one, including senior school pupils, secondary schoolteachers, and early undergraduate students. The activities reflect the different readerships; most can be suggested to all readers as ways of extending your understanding of the play and its historical and literary context. Some, such as the suggested comparison of Lyndsay's play with other morality plays and medieval farces, are more appropriate for undergraduate students.

Activity
Go to a personal computer and log onto Google Earth. Search for Cupar, Fife, and select the option that shows the names of the roads. Find where the Crossgate and Bonnygate meet. This is historically the centre of the town, where the medieval market was held. To the right you will see Castle Hill, which, for over a century before the play was written, was one of several locations where the medieval Scottish parliament had gathered. Castle Hill is where the first full version of the play was performed.

Then zoom out and see where Cupar is situated in relation to (i) St Andrews, the centre of the church that the play criticises so severely, (ii) to Linlithgow, which was the site of an earlier but much shorter version of the play, and (iii) to Edinburgh, the site of its third and final performance in the 16th century, and its first modern revival in 1948.

2. SIR DAVID LYNDSAY OF THE MOUNT (1486?–1555): HIS LIFE AND WORK

The records of David Lyndsay's early life are sketchy. He was born in or around 1486, the oldest of five sons of a small landowner whose properties lay in Fife and East Lothian. His father was also called David; the name of his mother is not known. One of his grandmothers, however, might have been the daughter of a burgess in Cupar, which would have given him a personal connection with the town that first staged the full version of his play. Little is known about his education. A David Lyndsay is listed amongst the graduates of St Andrews University in 1508–9, but we cannot be certain that this was the same man, especially since, at much the same time, another David Lyndsay is mentioned as being a groom in the stables of James IV. If it was the latter Lyndsay who later became the poet and dramatist, as seems likely, he would have witnessed many court entertainments, including tournaments and public performances of song and poetry – some of it by William Dunbar, a master of many styles ranging from religious and courtly celebration to frank comedy and biting satire. Certainly, references in Lyndsay's own later verse acknowledge his familiarity with and admiration for Dunbar's dazzling poetry.

Definite historical evidence about the man who wrote *Ane Satyre* dates from around 1511, when there is a note of payment to 'Dauid Lindesay' for a blue-and-yellow coat to be worn in the production of a play, performed before the king and queen. We do not know what the production was, but this is the earliest record of Lyndsay's active involvement in the dramatic culture of the Scottish court. Two years later, in 1513, however, James IV was dead on the battlefield of Flodden. In the wake of this disaster, Lyndsay found himself appointed as a companion and guardian to the infant, James V. Lyndsay occupied this role for ten years, until the king was twelve years of age. At this point, the child king was declared fit to rule, albeit under the control of Archibald Douglas, the Earl of Angus. In these turbulent political times, when different noble families fought for influence over the young monarch, Lyndsay temporarily lost his place as the king's companion. However, he seems to have remained at court, having married Janet Douglas, a woman who was seamstress to the king and related by family to the influential Earl of Angus.

During his years as the king's companion, Lyndsay began composing poetry. By the fifteenth century, the Scottish court had established itself as a forum in which courtiers like Dunbar and Lyndsay would write verse that circulated in manuscript and was often performed aloud at court events. Courtly poetry was generally written to celebrate such public occasions as holidays, marriages and funerals. As appropriate to the occasion, the poems were designed to amuse the king, queen and fellow courtiers with comic sketches of the life they shared, or to lead public celebration or mourning. Poets might use their talent to seek personal advancement, to dramatise conventional religious and moral values, and to criticise people or events of which they disapproved. Lyndsay's earliest known poem of any substance is *The Dreme* (c. 1526) in which the narrator is a servant who first reminds the king of his loyal service, and then of the rewards that should follow. The servant next describes a vision in which a lady, 'Dame Remembrance', takes him on an allegorical journey that in part relates historical events and the current state of Scotland to the moral actions of great leaders. In this early poem, we can see for the first time Lyndsay's concern with the positive and negative impact of a prudent or neglectful king on the common people of Scotland.

In 1528, at the age of 16, James V took personal control of the government, and he eventually reinstated Lyndsay as his companion. Shortly afterwards, Lyndsay took up a post as a herald, which meant that he began to organise and officiate at court events, and to participate in diplomatic missions to England, Belgium and France. This period is marked by two major poems, *The Complaynt* (c.1530), another poem that combines a plea for the poet's advancement with a sharp political commentary, and *The Testament of the Papyngo* (1530), supposedly the tragic-comic last words of the king's 'papyngo' or parrot. *The Testament of the Papyngo* can be read as a satirical illustration of the danger of refusing good advice, a theme that again surfaces strongly in *Ane Satyre of the Thrie Estaitis*.

The most significant of Lyndsay's diplomatic missions were trips to France, lasting up to eight months, undertaken as part of a series of negotiations that arranged the marriage of James V to Madeleine de Valois in 1536. To this period belongs a *Flyting* between Lyndsay and the king (c.1535–6). 'Flyting', or abusing an opponent in verse, is a long-established tradition in Scottish literary culture, and Lyndsay takes up the challenge, apparently offered by the king, as an opportunity to advise him to put his days of sexual promiscuity well behind him. The poem is further evidence of the degree of intimacy Lyndsay enjoyed in his relationship with James V, and his ease with his role as the king's adviser on moral and spiritual issues.

Given his evident interest and involvement in Scottish courtly culture, it is likely that Lyndsay took advantage of the opportunities of diplomatic travel to acquaint himself with the forms of entertainment performed in the courts he visited in continental Europe and England. Soon after James V's new queen arrived in Scotland from France, however, she became ill and died. In *The Deploratioun of the Deith of Quene Magdalene* (1537), a poem he wrote for her state funeral, Lyndsay refers poignantly to dramatic spectacles that had been arranged to welcome her to Scotland – celebratory performances that he himself may well have helped to devise.

A year after Madeleine's premature death, in 1537, James V took another noble French bride, Mary of Guise, the daughter of a prominent, influential and devout Catholic family. For Mary's arrival in Edinburgh, Lyndsay produced a theatrical pageant in which he played the part of a herald, advising the queen, as was the convention, to be obedient and virtuous. Lyndsay's continuing role as provider of occasional poems and entertainments for the court suggests that he was also responsible for a dramatic performance devised for the king and queen in the great hall of Linlithgow Palace, to celebrate Twelfth Night in 1540. In this entertainment, or 'interlude', a poor man, supported by the two temporal estates, the lords and merchants, complains about the oppression of the third estate, the church. The poor man does so in the presence of a fictional king, who has three courtiers, one of whom is called Placebo, another Flaterye. If Lyndsay did not actually write what is clearly an early version of *Ane Satyre of the Thrie Estaitis,* he was clearly strongly influenced by it when he later came to compose the fuller version. The text of this early play itself is now lost, and our knowledge of it comes only from notes taken by a member of the audience, which were later sent in a letter to Thomas Cromwell, the Lord Privy Seal of England. No doubt the political and religious sentiments of the play, and the Scottish king's enthusiastic response to it, were of urgent interest to the English court, and its king, Henry VIII. Scotland, which at this time was still a Catholic country, found itself increasingly torn between the two religious superpowers of Protestant England and Catholic France.

James V died in battle against an English army in 1542, at the age of 30, leaving Lyndsay with the sad task of organising his master and longstanding companion's funeral. After this, Lyndsay, now in his sixties, seems to have taken a less active role in court life, and he possibly spent more and more of his time in Fife, participating in the public administration of the burgh of Cupar. However, when in 1546 a group of Scottish Protestants murdered Cardinal Beaton in St Andrews Castle, it fell to Lyndsay, in his diplomatic role as Lord Lyon King of Arms, to negotiate the release of the castle governor's son, who had been taken hostage while the murderers awaited English assistance. Lyndsay's sympathies seem to have been mixed . He later wrote an ironic attack on Beaton, *The Tragedie of the Cardinall* (1547), a poem narrated by the murdered Cardinal's ghost. In late 1548 Lyndsay was again abroad on a diplomatic mission, this time to Denmark, another Protestant nation where Lyndsay would have encountered a vigorous initiative to translate the Bible into Danish. A poem, *Ane Dialog...of the Miserabyll Estait of the Warld,* possibly begun in the wake of his travels to Denmark, was a mixture of Biblical translation, religious history and commentary, and it became, on its publication in 1554, Lyndsay's best-known work in his own lifetime.

Otherwise, by the early 1550s, Lyndsay's work was associated much more closely with Fife. One of his finest later poems is a comic romance, *Squyer Meldrum* (c. 1550), based on the life and career of a local friend, William Meldrum of Cleish and Binns, who had recently died. And in June 1552, the full, expanded version of *Ane Satyre of the Thrie Estaitis* was performed in Cupar, with local in-jokes featuring alongside the broader references to Scottish life and politics. Although there is no firm evidence to support it, there is an agreeable tradition that Lyndsay himself took the part of Diligence, the hard-working herald, master of ceremonies and ironic commentator on the play's action. Diligence, crucially, has the first and last words in the play, and he complains amusingly at one point that he never yet has been paid for all his work. Alternatively, Lyndsay may have seen himself in the role of Gude Counsall, the honest adviser who is initially shunned by the young king. After the Cupar performance, the play was revised and performed again in August, 1554, in Edinburgh before a large crowd that included Mary of Guise. Lyndsay's death is recorded shortly thereafter, in a charter of March, 1555.

What in this summary of Lyndsay's life can illuminate our understanding of *Ane Satyre of the Thrie Estaitis*? First of all, the play is a satire on contemporary social, political and religious issues, composed with the knowledge of an insider – someone who was at the heart of the Scottish court for much of his life, and who experienced its triumphs and turbulence first-hand. Secondly, it is a play written by someone who was exposed both to the flowering of Scottish poetry in the court of James IV, who participated actively in poetry and theatrical spectacles devised for court occasions, and who travelled widely and often enough to compare Scottish ideas and culture with those current in Belgium, Denmark, England and France. His own literary works, from start to finish, show that Lyndsay combined a deep knowledge of Scottish literary culture with a first-hand exposure to other cultures. Even if the playwright was not the David Lyndsay who attended

St Andrews University, he nevertheless learned much about Scottish and European literature and performance from direct experience and active participation. Thirdly, Lyndsay lived through interesting times. He saw two Scottish kings cut down in their prime, and was a close companion to the second through much of his early childhood. He was a diplomat, often engaged in international negotiations on peace, marriage and religious affairs. Occasionally he found himself caught up in incidents of domestic terrorism in an increasingly bitter sectarian conflict. Yet he could not wholly be claimed by either side in Scotland's developing religious war. While his writing criticises corruption in the ranks of the Catholic Church, he never abandons his belief in reform rather than revolution. His sojourn in Protestant Denmark clearly influenced his religious beliefs, although *Ane Satyre of the Thrie Estaites* combines a call for clerical reform with an affirmation that the affairs of church and state should be clearly separate. Crucially, though the small landowner's son became Sir David Lyndsay of the Mount, Lord Lyon King of Arms, a distinguished courtier, diplomat, poet and playwright, he never lost his sympathy with the common folk, the tailors and cobblers and paupers who made up the majority of the Scottish population. His attitude to their wives is more debateable; his writing is characterised by frequently unfavourable descriptions of women as nagging, cunning and sexually promiscuous. In this he draws uncritically on misogynist traditions of medieval and renaissance farce. His virtuous women are relatively passive mouthpieces for the qualities they represent. As we shall see, modern adaptors and translators of Lyndsay's play now often address his negative representation of women by changing the gender of the valiant spokesman for ordinary folk from 'John' to 'Jane the Common-weill'.

While Lyndsay was evidently a reformer who sympathised with the peasants and tradesmen, it would be anachronistic to think of him as a democrat. His vision of social harmony constituted a hierarchy of king, nobility, merchants and churchmen, all attending to the material and spiritual needs of the common folk. To act otherwise would be an offence to God.

Activity

Using historical reference materials, from a library or from the web, draw a timeline of the main political events in Scotland from 1480–1560. The timeline should include events such as the birth, marriage and death of monarchs such as James IV, James V and Mary, Queen of Scots, as well as episodes like the Battle of Flodden, the Battle of Solway Moss, and the establishment of the Presbyterian Church of Scotland. Onto your timeline add events from the life of David Lyndsay, such as his birth, the publication of his major works, and his diplomatic missions. (A sample timeline is given at the end of this Scotnote.)

3. THE HISTORY OF THE TEXT

Book culture in the early 16th century was very different from book culture today. The earliest printing press in Scotland was set up by two publishers, Chapman and Myllar, in 1508, when Lyndsay was about 21. The press was mainly established so that the Acts of Parliament, the laws of Scotland that had been decreed by the Three Estates, could be published and disseminated among the people whose lives they were designed to regulate. For many decades afterwards, however, much Scottish literature was still recorded in manuscripts which were laboriously copied out and held in private libraries, or circulated amongst small groups of friends. Since much early Scottish literature only existed in limited manuscript editions, untold numbers of poems and plays are probably now lost for ever. Despite his public prominence and acknowledged literary skills, most of Lyndsay's work had to wait until after his death to find its way into print. Indeed, *Ane Satyre of the Thrie Estaitis* illustrates the shift from manuscript to print culture that characterises Scottish literature towards the end of the 16th century.

As noted in the previous section, the satirical drama performed in Linlithgow Palace in January 1540, as part of the court's Twelfth Night celebrations in the presence of James V and Mary of Guise, was probably an early version of Lyndsay's play. No copy of this version of the play survives beyond the descriptive notes jotted down by an audience member who was effectively acting as an spy for the English court. The earliest copy of the much later 1552 version of the play, performed in Cupar, is in the priceless collection of early Scottish literary texts that was compiled in manuscript by an Edinburgh merchant, George Bannatyne. This collection dates from about 1558, and it survives as 'The Bannatyne Manuscript' in the National Library of Scotland. Had it perished, our knowledge of early Scottish literature would be immeasurably poorer. The version of *Ane Satyre of the Thrie Estaites* that was copied by hand into the Bannatyne Manuscript has, however, been adapted for reading rather than performance. The sequence of episodes has been rearranged, and the play has been abridged, running to 3377 lines.

The earliest print edition of the play was published by Robert Charteris, in Edinburgh, as late as 1602, fifty years after the Cupar performance and one year before James V's grandson, James VI of Scotland, became James I of the United Kingdom. The Charteris edition is 4630 lines long, and it seems to be a complete version of the play-text of the Cupar performance of 1552. Most modern editions therefore take the Charteris version as a 'copy text'; that is, most modern editors use it as the basis for new editions of the play. Only seven copies of the original Charteris edition survive, two of which were reprints that were published in London, with a new title page, in 1604. Clearly, fifty years after its performance, the play's theme of a new king coming of age and addressing the neglect of his people's spiritual and material needs was again a timely one in Scotland and England, just before and after the accession of James VI of Scotland to the English throne. Even among these seven surviving copies published by Charteris, there are some variant readings, since the text seems to have been corrected during its print run. Most modern editors therefore compare each line of the surviving different print versions from 1602 (and the 1604 reprints) with the Bannatyne manuscript version of around 1568, to arrive at what is called a 'critical edition'. The edition that you might be reading, therefore, can be thought of as an expert archaeological reconstruction of the original play-text.

However, several modern editions of the play do not aim at an accurate rendition of the 16th century text. In 1948, the organisers of the newly established Edinburgh International Festival wished to include in their programme something with a particularly Scottish theme. As a consequence, the playwright and BBC radio producer, Robert Kemp, was commissioned to provide a celebrated theatre director, Tyrone Guthrie, with a play script that reduced and reworked Lyndsay's version, omitting various scenes and conflating characters. The production was a critical and popular triumph, and its fame was such that Kemp's acting version was adapted and published by literary scholar, Matthew McDiarmid, in

1967. This version has been the basis for several theatrical revivals, perhaps most successfully in 1984 and 1991 under the direction of Tom Fleming. In 1998, Nigel Mace, whose own love of the play was inspired by seeing it performed in Edinburgh when he was five years old, translated an acting version into English, cutting some of Kemp's scenes and restoring others. More recently, Lyndsay's older Scots version has been abridged and updated by Alan Spence as *The 3 Estaites: The Millennium Version.* As noted above, an interesting and apparently enduring innovation in recent productions, perhaps inspired by a brief extract broadcast by the Open University in the 1990s, has been to change the gender of the character of John the Common-weill to Jane the Common-weill, a prominent role for the actress Gerda Stevenson in the production of Alan Spence's version. A more detailed discussion of modern performances and versions is given, alongside a consideration of the play's broader impact on Scottish drama, towards the end of this Scotnote.

It is crucial to understand something of the textual history of the play because it highlights several issues that are important to consider at the outset of any serious engagement with it. One is how to determine the essence of any literary text that is primarily designed for performance. Written records appear relatively stable and fixed, whereas dramatic renditions change according to the dynamics of each and every staging. The different written versions of *Ane Satyre of the Thrie Estaitis* are frozen artefacts from very different periods of Scottish cultural history:

- an age when printed versions were a newfangled novelty, and a manuscript version could be trimmed to reflect an individual reader's taste;
- an age when readers north and south of the border were interested in seeing how a fictional Scottish king might respond to religious turmoil and strife;
- an age when the value of a fragile Scottish dramatic tradition needed to be reaffirmed and positioned at the heart of a new cultural festival in Edinburgh;

- an age when the play had come to be seen as the foundation of a golden era of Scottish drama;
- an age when the older Scots tradition was updated, re-gendered, and 'taken home' to the community that gave it birth.

Each written version of the play also acts as a blueprint for a whole multitude of actual performances, every one of which will further rework the play to meet the demands of a particular group of players, a certain director, the constraints of a budget, the peculiarities of the venue, the ever-changing dynamics of the audience, and even, when it is played in the open air, the weather. Even so, some things remain constant. Both in its written forms and in its many actualisations as performance, the play engages the contemporary reader or spectator in a conversation with Scotland's past – a dialogue about the moral basis of our personal relationships, our social structures and our religious and political institutions.

No doubt the continuing need for the present to have a dramatic dialogue with the past will result in new versions of this oldest of Scottish plays. Sir David Lyndsay's enduring legacy is destined to live on.

Activity

Check your copy of the play for the editor's comments on the version used as a basis for the edition. Are you using a 'critical edition' or a more popular abridgement? Has Lyndsay's language been updated in any way? What can you expect from different kinds of edition? How are the different types of edition likely to shape your own response to the play? If you have access to two or more editions, compare some key scenes. Read the introduction to each edition; then compare and contrast the editor's statement of his or her intention in presenting the play as he or she has. Further information about different versions is given later, in Section 11 below.

4. *DRAMATIS PERSONÆ*

Before summarising the plot of *Ane Satyre of the Thrie Estaitis,* it is worth commenting upon the *dramatis personae*, or the characters in the drama. It is helpful to do this before considering the plot, since most of the characters in Lyndsay's play do not meet modern expectations. Modern audiences attending a play tend to expect to encounter well-rounded characters, whose role is to dramatise a complex mixture of personal strengths and weaknesses, perhaps exposed by an externally-imposed crisis. In many dramatisations, we expect such complex characters to proceed through a narrative arc, perhaps of self-discovery, to reach a resolution. For example, the hero of John Byrne's *The Slab Boys* can be seen as a talented character with relatively little confidence and limited employment prospects, driven finally and painfully to reject his peers and their low expectations, and in so doing to become an artist. As we watch such a character develop on stage, we may alternate in our response between sympathy and criticism, or self-recognition and loathing. However, in *Ane Satyre of the Thrie Estaitis,* the characters embody one particular virtue or vice, or represent a moral – or immoral – set of beliefs. With one important exception, that of King Humanitie, they do not develop, or follow a narrative arc. This kind of play offers a different kind of pleasure – that of the recognition of stereotypes, and the playing out of a familiar drama in which the forces of evil get their comeuppance from the forces of good. In the time of its first production, this familiar drama of good versus evil would affirm a set of religious beliefs with roots in the Christian faith. The drama would be given a twist by the fact that many of the characters embodying evil are shown to be exploiting a very particular set of legal practices and customs that would have been painfully familiar to the audience in Cupar. And so, to gain a victory over the forces of evil, the forces of good have to adopt a specific set of political and religious reforms that the Scottish parliament had, at the time of the play, yet to confirm. This immediate political relevance gave a familiar story a unique edge.

The Cupar Banns, which were acted out in advance as an advertisement for the performance of the full play in June 1552, contain several characters who are similar but not identical to characters in the play itself: **Nuntius,** a herald whose role is to make announcements; a **Cottar** and his **Wyfe** whose strained marital relations preview that of the Sowtar ('Cobbler'); a boastful but cowardly soldier, **Fynlaw of the Fute Band**; a jealous **Auld Man** with his promiscuous young wife, **Bessy**, who is forced to wear a chastity belt; members of the Three Estates, an equally lustful **Marchand** ('Merchant'), **Courteour** and **Clerk,** all of whom try but fail to free Bessy from her chastity belt while her husband is asleep; and a clever **Fule** ('Fool'), not unlike Foly in the main play, who succeeds in freeing her, seducing her, and tricking both her husband and the cowardly soldier. The characters in the Cupar Banns thus introduce some of the themes that will re-appear in the play itself – deception and self-deception across a wide social spectrum. The emphasis in this preview is on broad sexual comedy, presumably to attract as wide as possible an audience to the Castle Hill on the 7th of June.

In the play proper, **Rex Humanitas** (King Humanitie) is the one character whose storyline allows for change. He is a relatively complex character for a play of this period in that he is both representative of all people (he stands for all 'Humanitie') and yet he is a specific individual (*Rex*, 'the king'). When we first encounter him, he is young and innocent, practically a schoolboy. Some commentators have associated King Humanitie with the young James V, whose guardian Lyndsay was for many years. While the portrayal of the fictional king might well have been inspired by Lyndsay's friendship with the real monarch as a youth (and we understand from Lyndsay's other work that James fell prey to Sensualitie, at least before his marriages) it is difficult to draw a direct parallel, since Humanitie's story follows the conventional path of the hero of a morality play.

King Humanitie first describes himself to the audience using a Latin phrase, *tanquam tabula rasa* ('like a smooth, wax writing tablet') – that is, he is unwritten upon by experience, and so 'ready for good or ill' (lines 224–6). As a representative of all humanity, he follows a general narrative plot that Christianity has outlined from the time of Adam and Eve onwards. That is, Humanitie begins in innocence, then he is seduced by worldly temptations that are symbolised by 'Dame Sensualitie'. As a consequence, his kingdom suffers, before he is redeemed by heavenly intervention, in the shape, here, of Divyne Correctioun. King Humanitie emerges from this process wiser and more experienced. At this point, his story begins to correspond less to the general story of a representative Everyman, and it aligns more specifically with that of a king. Having been reformed by Divyne Correctioun, King Humanitie listens to advisers who are honest and good, rather than foolish and self-serving. Thus, he is able to lead the Three Estates in reforming the laws of the Scotland, in order to restore social and moral harmony to the nation. There was in medieval and renaissance Scotland – and arguably there still is, in Scotland and beyond – a profound need to project onto the leader of the nation a set of values that represent the nation at its finest. In much early literature, there is a common theme that a morally corrupt king will result in a morally corrupt kingdom; a virtuous king is therefore a prerequisite for social and moral harmony.

The Vices fall into three main groups, all characterised most obviously by their names, all of which indicate abstract moral qualities. First, we have the male courtiers, from the ringleader, **Wantonnes** (i.e. 'Someone who loves or acts without thinking of the consequences'), to the cheerfully easygoing and corruptible **Placebo** (i.e. 'Someone who pleases, or sucks up to another') and the helplessly drunk **Solace** (i.e. 'Someone who cheers or comforts'). Next, we have their female counterparts, the sexually promiscuous courtesan, **Dame Sensualitie** and her three attendants: **Hamelines** (i.e. 'Plainness'), probably a drab prostitute, the seductive and sexually avaricious **Danger** (which at this time could mean something like 'Someone who plays hard-to-get'), and **Fund-Jonet** (or 'Janet the foundling', a woman who was abandoned as a child). 'Fund-Jonet' was possibly the nickname of a real woman in James V's court; given her impoverished circumstances, the character might be a brothel-keeper.

The third group of vices is attracted to the court by the seduction of the king by Sensualitie. The most important of these vices is **Flatterie**, a key character in the play, one who preys on the fact that others are capable of self-deception and corruption. Flatterie is a character who thrives on deception and betrayal; on the medieval stage he wore 'motley' or many-coloured clothes to represent his unreliability. His companions are the stupid **Falset** ('Falsehood') and the more cunning **Dissait** ('Deceit'). There are also several other vices such as **Oppressioun** and **Common Thift** ('Common Theft'). Towards the end of the play we also encounter the slightly more ambiguous vice, **Foly** ('Folly'), with his two children, **Glaiks** and **Stult** (both terms suggesting 'foolish person'). Some later productions conflate the characters of Flatterie and Foly; however, the latter character is an important one in one medieval dramatic tradition that suggests human beings are ultimately driven by folly. Foly's appearance at the end of the play is a half-serious, half-comic reminder that the high-minded reforms suggested in the play will have to contend with humanity's inherent foolishness.

Since the characters all represent moral abstractions, it is important that members of the audience quickly and clearly recognise who they are. Accordingly, if you read lines 102–189 you will see that much of the early dialogue is taken up with the vices introducing themselves and each other, and identifying themselves with their characteristic behaviour: Wantonnes first introduces King Humanitie to Placebo with the promise that they will be merry; they then seek the absent Solace, who eventually arrives in a typically drunken state. Their characters are therefore immediately defined and established. Lines 271–326 mark the entrance of Sensualitie and her ladies; again Sensualitie begins by identifying herself and her typical characteristics, and then the dialogue between her attendants makes plain to the audience who they are too. Taken together, these are the villains of the play: each of the vices represents an aspect of the human character that is sinful or which leads to sin. And it is Flatterie who gets the best lines, the loudest laughs, and who is allowed to escape hanging in the end.

The Virtues are equally static characters, defined by their names, **Chastitie, Veritie** ('Truth'), **Gude Counsall** and **Divyne Correctioun**. The main virtues and vices fall into opposing groups in the moral universe of the play: the pure Chastitie is set against the king's wanton courtiers, Dame Sensualitie and her promiscuous ladies; the truthful Veritie is in contrast to Falset and Dissait; and the honest and reliable Gude Counsall opposes Flatterie. However, Divyne Correctioun has no direct counterpart; he acts as a *deus ex machina,* a direct ambassador from God, appearing miraculously in Scotland to put right the kingdom's wrongs. Like the vices, the virtues are creatures of allegory, a common medieval literary form in which stories unfold as extended metaphors. The metaphor in this case is of the fall and redemption of man. The dramatic function of the virtues and vices is not to develop believable flesh-and-blood characters but simply to be what they are, namely representatives of the side of good or evil.

If the vices and virtues are less human beings and more abstract tokens of good and evil, the 'people' in the play are also less individuals and more representatives of social groups. Even King Humanitie combines a unique personage, the king, with his representative function as 'Everyman'. The general drama of human redemption is heightened by the fact that when it is a king who falls from grace, the entire kingdom suffers as a consequence. King Humanitie's individual spiritual recuperation is attended by a very specific set of political reforms that improve the welfare of the lowest in the kingdom.

The Three Estates themselves are represented by a range of characters. Two characters speak for the temporal, or secular, ranks of lords and merchants: **Temporalitie,** despite his name, speaks largely for the nobility alone, and there is also a **Merchand** who speaks for his class. On the whole, Lyndsay presents the temporal Estates as open to reform. Once Divyne Correctioun arrives and the oppression of ordinary people has been revealed by John the Common-weill, King Humanitie, the lords and merchants all agree to reform very quickly. Although capable of corruption and neglect, they have a fundamental decency. The real opposition to reform is found in the third Estate, the spiritual counterpart to the two secular Estates, namely, the church.

Spiritualitie is a senior member of the church, often characterised as a bishop who speaks for the clergy as a whole. There are also lesser but equally corrupt church officials: an **Abbot,** an **Abbasse** (Abbess), a **Persone** (Parson), a **Priores** and a **Pardoner**. These members of the spiritual Estate are the main targets of Lyndsay's satire. Several key scenes are concerned with showing members of the clergy to be hypocritical, lecherous, and greedy for wealth and power. The individual members portray different ranks within the church, from the lustful bishop to the wandering Pardoner, who travels with his young apprentice, **Wilkin**. Together, they sell the foolish and gullible pardons for their sins, and dupe them into believing that horse and cattle bones are the valuable relics of famous saints, or even of characters from secular legends. For suitable payment, and in a grotesque ceremony, the Pardoner will even release unhappy couples from the bonds of marriage that his creed is supposed to hold sacred.

Despite the obstinacy of these churchmen and churchwomen of senior and lowly status in grasping for worldly power and privilege, Lyndsay does not portray the entire Catholic church as beyond salvation. When Divyne Correctioun and King Humanitie send forth for learned clergymen, the herald manages to find and bring to court three learned and worthy, if rather earnest, clergymen and lawyers, a **Doctour** and **First** and **Second Licent** whose combined scriptural knowledge and ability to preach is contrasted with the shallow ignorance of their so-called superiors. Furthermore, the revelation of the Abbasse's earlier suffering at the hands of her family, made as she revokes her cloistered life in favour of that of a wife, evokes one of the play's more sympathetic responses to a woman. In the end, *Ane Satyre of the Thrie Estaitis* calls not for the disbandment of the Catholic Church, to which key moral characters pledge their continuing allegiance, but it does call for a set of criteria to be established and enforced that will determine the clergy's fitness to hold clerical office.

A Satire of the Three Estates

The common folk who suffer and endure have as their spokesman **John the Common-weill**. John breaks into the assembly of the Estates to plead the case of the ordinary, persecuted subject; in doing so with dignity, eloquence, pride and natural authority, he is the Scottish democratic spirit made flesh. Through this character, Lyndsay affirms his sympathetic attachment to the ordinary folk whose livelihood and security the laws of the realm were supposed to protect. John the Common-weill's complaint to the Three Estates transforms the spiritual authorities and secular lords from exploiters to protectors of the common people. The lowest ranks in society are even held up as examples to their social superiors: the clergy are exhorted to be as skilled in scripture and preaching as Taylours and Sowtars are at their craft. The character of John is not recorded in the surviving description of the earliest version of the play. The notes on this performance do mention a **Pauper** ('poor man') who, in the later Cupar play-text, becomes a companion to John, and an example of someone whose wretched luck and cruel exploitation by members of the clergy have left him struggling at the very bottom of the social hierarchy.

However, the lower ranks of society do not escape Lyndsay's satirical eye. The **Sowtar** and **Taylour** and their respective **Wives** represent the tradition of farce that *Ane Satyre of the Thrie Estaitis* also draws upon. Although the men are skilled in their craft, and despite the fact that they show hospitality to Chastitie when she seeks their aid, they rail against the conventions of marriage, and are nagged at and dominated by their wives. The wives, for their part, exhibit conventional traits of women in medieval comedy – a combination of suspicion and gross sexual appetite. Alerted by the Taylour's tell-tale daughter, **Jennie**, that the men are entertaining a beautiful young woman, the wives drive Chastitie away, ironically believing her to be a prostitute. And, in a near-blasphemous scene often cut from modern editions and performances, the Sowtar and his wife undergo a parodic divorce ceremony, supervised by the Pardoner, that involves one kissing the other's arse.

There are some minor characters, such as the **Page** who announces the arrival of Divyne Correctioun, and a **Scrybe** who records the proceedings of the parliament. A **First** and **Second Sergeant** are called to arrest the vices and administer justice. But the main master of ceremonies is **Diligence,** the king's herald. As we have seen, Lyndsay himself became a senior herald in the service of James V, and his duties as such were varied, from acting as a diplomat abroad, to organising court celebrations and officiating at royal events at home. Heralds — such as the Lord Lyon King of Arms — still exist today, but their duties are largely confined to performing at official engagements, or granting coats of arms to people or institutions who claim honourable service of one kind or another. As Lord Lyon King of Arms, Lyndsay wrote the first Scottish guide to the science of heraldry. In the play Diligence calls the audience to order, obeys the king's commandments, and sums up the proceedings. For a potentially stock character, he is a humorous and human figure, attentive to the hunger and thirst of the audience members, and their need to relieve their bladders from time to time. At the end of the play he pleads for the audience's tolerance of the potentially 'odious' contents of the play, an appeal which was probably more than a conventional theatrical gesture, since this was a time when writers could be banished or even executed for articulating such critical views as Lyndsay expressed.

These then, are the characters who populate the social panorama that is Lyndsay's Scotland in the mid 16th century. It was a time of common people standing up for themselves in the face of centuries of institutional persecution by church and state. But if it was a time of terror, it was also a time of belly laughs. Sexual comedy played off against statutory reforms, in a play of princes, priests, prostitutes, pratfalls and providence.

A Satire of the Three Estates

Activity
Look at the first speeches of different characters in the play. Which contemporary actors would you cast in the main roles – and why? Who would you cast as a naïve King Humanitie, a deceptive and cunning Flatterie, a seductive Dame Sensualite, an upright Divyne Correctioun? How would you dress the characters in the play? Would you go for modern dress, or would you go for period costume? Look at the photographs and costume designs in this Scotnote, which are taken from productions of the play. If you have the opportunity, look at more photographs of the play on the Scottish Cultural Resources Access Network at **www.scran.ac.uk** – or look for photographs and drawings from other morality plays on Google Images. (You will need to enter different spellings of the play – 'thrie estaitis' 'three estates', 'three estaites', etc.) Can you identify the characters from their dress alone? Think about how words and images combine to symbolise moral character on the stage.

The next section gives a detailed summary of the fullest version of the play, the 1552 play-text, with line numbers taken from Professor Roderick Lyall's critical edition, published by Canongate.

5. A SUMMARY OF THE PLAY

Proclamatioun maid in Cowpar of Fyffe
Some days before the performance of the play in Cupar, some of the players performed some sketches to advertise the event. The sketches are known as the 'Cupar Banns' or the 'Cupar Proclamation'. The Cupar Banns help to date the full performance as taking place on the Tuesday after Whitsuntide, 7th June, in 1552. The Cupar Banns are sometimes included as an appendix in editions of the play. The 1552 text is not divided into scenes, as in a modern play-text, so the line divisions below simply follow episodes in the plot.

[1–100]: A herald ['Nuntius'] addresses the audience, and proclaims the imminent arrival of a prince who will convene a parliament of the Three Estates. It will happen on the seventh day of June, weather permitting, and begin at seven in the morning on Castle Hill. He urges the audience to attend. A Cottar, or small farmer, announces that he will be present, with his drinking companion. He then complains to the herald about his wife, whom he would like to divorce. The herald asks him if he wishes to re-marry; the Cottar replies that he does not; he would prefer to live like abbots, monks, friars and priests, who engage in sexual relations without bothering about marriage. The Cottar's wife appears and scolds him, telling him that he will stay at home, minding the cattle, while she attends the play. The Cottar and his Wife then argue and she beats him physically.

[101–141]: A soldier enters and complains about the disturbance. He identifies himself to the audience as Fynlaw of the Fute Band, and boasts of his exploits in battle. He then lies down to rest, at which point a Fule ('fool') enters, recognises the sleeping soldier as a notorious coward, and resolves to trick him with a sheep's head before he departs.

[142–175]: An Auld Man enters with his young wife, Bessy, whose fidelity he guarantees by locking her in a chastity belt. He lies down to sleep, with Bessy beside him. She is visited

A Satire of the Three Estates

by a member of each of the Three Estates – a courtier, a merchant and a religious clerk – all of whom attempt to seduce her. The Fule follows in their wake, and, though Bessy would yield to his seduction, she draws his attention to the belt. The Fule steals the key from the sleeping Auld Man, and he and Bessy go to a quiet place.

[176–207]: Fynlaw awakes and announces that he seeks people to travel with him to the war in France, where he is captain of a hundred spearsmen. The religious clerk rebukes him, observing that his cowardice was apparent at a past battle, and that the commonwealth suffers from such warmongers such himself. They argue and the clerk departs, hoping to see him hanged. Fynlaw tells the audience that he was just about to hack the clerk's head off with his sword.

[208–237]: The commotion wakes the Auld Man, who sees that Bessy has gone and also that he has lost the key to her chastity belt. He laments his woes, and Bessy returns, with a new shirt for him. As she puts the shirt over his head, the Fule secretly returns the key. When the Auld Man asks Bessy where the key is, she shows that it is safe where he lay his head, sleeping. The Auld Man apologises for having suspected her.

[238–269]: Fynlaw begins another speech, again boasting of his brave exploits in war. As he warms to his theme, the Fule enters, with a sheep's head on a staff, appearing to be a monster. Fynlaw is terrified, surrenders immediately and pleads for mercy.

[270–277]: The herald returns and addresses the audience again, urging them to rise early on Whitsun Tuesday, have a good breakfast and relieve themselves, and then come to see the play.

Part One
The first part of the play charts the fall into sin of an individual who, as king, is also God's representative on earth. We meet

King Humanitie, an inexperienced young monarch of Scotland. Although he announces his intention to rule wisely, he is surrounded by weak courtiers who lead him into the path of Dame Sensualitie and her attendant vices. Once the King has been seduced by Sensualitie, other vices, such as Flatterie, Dissait and Falset, run riot in the kingdom, disguising themselves as holy men and banishing honest advisers such as Gude Counsall, and imprisoning the virtues Veritie and Chastitie.

[1–77]: Diligence, a herald, introduces the play, previewing the main events, which will involve the seduction of Rex Humanitas (King Humanitie) by sensual vices, and his eventual reformation by Divyne Correctioun and the virtues, Veritie and Chastitie.

[78–101]: King Humanitie enters and introduces himself: he is a young, inexperienced monarch with good intentions. He prays that he will not be swayed by temptation.

[102–553]: Despite the king's intentions, however, the courtiers Wantones, Placebo and Solace engineer a meeting between the young king and Dame Sensualitie, who has arrived in Scotland with her attendants, Hamelines, Danger and Fund-Jonet. The king falls under Sensualitie's spell.

[554–601]: Gude Counsall, an honest adviser, enters and introduces himself to the audience: he has been exiled from Scotland, and has been travelling in England, Italy and France. He has returned to Scotland to rescue the king from the counsellors who have corrupted him for their own benefit.

[602–807]: Also returned from the continent is the vice, Flatterie, with his companions Falset (Falsehood) and Dissait (Deceit). This trio of vices has arrived to take advantage of Scotland's descent into corruption. They disguise themselves as holy men, and take the names of virtues: Flatterie styles himself as Devotioun, Falset disguises himself as Sapience

A Satire of the Three Estates

(Wisdom), and Dissait pretends to be Discretioun. After a mock baptism to confirm their new names, they seek out the king.

[808–937]: The king and his courtiers enter and praise the pleasures of love-making. The three disguised vices approach the king and ingratiate themselves with him.

[938–1033]: The vices prevent Gude Counsall from gaining access to the king, and they banish him from the realm. In his absence, the three vices resolve to share any vacant religious offices, and their profits, between themselves.

[1034–1199]: The virtue, Veritie, enters, seeking King Humanitie. Her arrival is observed by the three vices, who persuade Spiritualitie, a senior churchman, and his attendant Abbot and Persone (Parson) to arrest her on false charges, and put her in the stocks, which they do.

[1200–1395]: Another virtue, Chastitie, enters, bewailing her banishment from the secular and spiritual Estates, and her exile from the company of princes. She encounters Diligence, who recommends that she seek out 'ladies of religion', that is, nuns. However, the nuns reject her, as do Spiritualitie, the Abbot, the Persone, and a noble representative of the two secular Estates. She is temporarily given shelter by two common people, a Taylour (Tailor) and a Sowtar (Soutar, or Cobbler). However, the Taylour's daughter, Jennie, tells her mother that her father is drinking with a beautiful young woman, and the wives of the Taylour and Sowtar drive Chastitie away. Having soundly scolded their husbands, the two wives resolve to make merry.

[1396–1481]: Chastitie again encounters Diligence, who this time advises her to seek out the king. As she approaches the king, one of his attendants, Solace, alerts him to the fact that a beautiful young woman is approaching. Before she can arrive, Dame Sensualitie intervenes and commands Dissait to imprison Chastitie in the stocks alongside Veritie. Veritie comforts Chastitie by telling her that she has heard that Divyne Correctioun is newly landed and will protect them from further harm.

[1482–1579]: The servant of Divyne Correctioun enters and announces his master's intention to gather and reform the Three Estates. Dissait resolves to flee to the merchant class, while Flatterie decides to seek protection with Spiritualitie. Falset, in turn, takes refuge amongst the craftsmen of the country. Before they go, the three vices steal a box of treasure from the king. However, they argue about who will take the greatest share of the king's treasure. In the resultant scuffle, Falset loses an eye and Dissait makes off with the box.

[1580–1676]: Divyne Correctioun arrives and tells the audience that he intends to convene a parliament of the Three Estates. He explains the duties expected by God of a king, and his own role as God's judge. He is welcomed by Gude Counsall, who appeals to him to free Veritie and Chastitie from the stocks. Divyne Correctioun is surprised that Gude Counsall has been banished from the king's presence, and he liberates Veritie and Chastitie. The two virtues appeal to him to go to the king and rescue him from the clutches of Dame Sensualitie.

[1677–1784]: As Divyne Correctioun comes nearer the king, he is watched apprehensively by the courtiers, Wantones, Placebo and Solace. They try to waken the king, who is sleeping with Dame Sensualitie. Sensualitie scolds the courtiers for daring to disturb the king; however, she is silenced by the arrival of Divyne Correctioun. Correctioun wakens the king and reminds him of the catastrophes that occurred when earlier rulers, in the bible, history and legend, fell prey to sensuality. The king demands to know the source of Divyne Correctioun's authority; Divyne Correctioun responds by banishing Dame Sensualitie from the king's presence. She meekly submits, pleading to be allowed to go to Rome. Taking her leave of King Humanitie, she is received into the company of Spiritualitie – the bishops and cardinals eagerly welcome her and her attendants with kisses. Divyne Correc-

A Satire of the Three Estates

tioun then recommends Gude Counsall, Veritie and Chastitie to the king, reminding him again of the fate of rulers who turn to a vice-ridden life. Now King Humanitie submits to Divyne Correctioun's command, and they embrace.

[1785–1909]: Divyne Correctioun then directs King Humanitie to convene a parliament of the Three Estates, to address the country's problems by reforming the law. King Humanitie sends Diligence to gather Spiritualitie and the two temporal Estates together, and Diligence departs, complaining to the audience that he has never yet been paid for all this work. Correctioun summons the king's courtiers, Wantones, Placebo and Solace, and threatens to punish them for leading the king into temptation. The courtiers defend themselves by observing that lechery is widely practised, both at home and abroad, by princes and prioresses. Divyne Correctioun pardons the courtiers on condition that, in future, they entertain the king with 'lawful' distractions such as hawking, hunting, and activities that will serve to prepare him for battle. The king asks the whereabouts of Discretioun, Sapience and Devotioun; Veritie and Chastitie inform him that these three apparent virtues were in fact vices in disguise. These vices were responsible for imprisoning the two virtues and also for stealing the king's box. The king then turns to Gude Counsall for better advice on how to rule. Gude Counsall directs the king to remember that he is the mortal instrument of God, and that his first duty is to see that justice is equally served to all his subjects. He should mix justice with mercy, but without special favour. He recommends that the king study history, since by doing so he will learn the good and evil qualities of past rulers.

[1910–1933]: Diligence returns and proclaims that the parliament of the Three Estates will convene – and he exhorts the audience to have a drink and relieve themselves before the start of the second part of the play.

Interlude
The interlude serves to allow the members of the audience to do as Diligence suggests, namely attend to their physical

needs. However, for those that remain during the interlude, a number of comic episodes are played that indicate the state of social and spiritual unrest in the country.

[1934–2086]: First, out of the crowd there appears a Pauper, who begins to beg for alms, much to the irritation of Diligence. The Pauper climbs on the king's throne and argues with Diligence, who tries to make him leave. At last, the Pauper tells Diligence how he has come to be a poor beggar: when his parents and wife died, the laird and church laid claim to his horse and cattle as death duty, making him and his children destitute. He now seeks some kind of compensation from the law, an aspiration that Diligence treats with scepticism.

[2087–2186]: Diligence exits, the Pauper lies down to rest, and a Pardoner enters, advertising to the audience that he is selling pardons for sin. He is also selling relics of legendary and holy figures, such as a piece of the rope that hanged the notorious raider, John Armstrong, and the rump of Saint Bride's cow. The Sowtar makes an appearance, and asks the Pardoner for a divorce from his wife. The Sowtar's wife enters and threatens her husband. The Pardoner asks her if she would agree to a divorce; when she does, the Pardoner announces that he will grant a separation if each partner kisses the other's arse. They do so, and the Pardoner sends them happily on their way.

[2187–2300]: A boy, the Pardoner's assistant, enters and tells the Pardoner that he has been collecting animal bones that will serve as 'relics'. He then gives the Pardoner news of his anticipated reception in the village; their discussion wakes the Pauper who seeks the Pardoner's help in the recovery of his cattle. For a groat (a trifling sum of money), the Pardoner sells him a thousand years of pardons for his sins; the Pauper realises that he has been duped and attempts to recover his money. They fight, and in the commotion the Pardoner's relics are thrown into the water. Diligence reappears and has both of them sent to prison, to be hanged when the play is over.

A Satire of the Three Estates

Part Two
The second part of the play is concerned with the reformations that will restore moral and social order to the nation after the 'fall' of King Humanitie in Part One. Divyne Correctioun convenes a parliament of the Three Estates, Spiritualitie (the church) and Temporalitie (the lords and merchants). Spiritualitie is shown to be the most resistant to change; however, its hypocrisies are gradually exposed and, after the proclamation of Acts of Parliament that will reform the country, the vices that have led to moral disorder are eventually punished by banishment or death. Afterwards, however, a fool enters and preaches a mock sermon that shows how folly remains characteristic of all levels of society, from monarchs on down.

[2301–2358]: Diligence makes a proclamation that begins the second part of the play, announcing the arrival of the Three Estates that make up the parliament. A procession of the lords, merchants and clergy appears – however, they walk backwards, a shameful act that symbolises both their lack of respect for the king's summons and the moral and social confusion that besets the nation. The courtiers, Wantones, Placebo and Solace, arrive in court in advance of the procession, and hasten to alert the king to the scandal. Gude Counsall advises the king to let Divyne Correctioun attend to the matter, after which he will be in a position to reform the wrongdoers.

[2359–2497]: The leaders of the Three Estates, Spiritualitie (representing the clergy), Temporalitie (representing the nobility) and a Marchand (merchant) arrive and turn towards the King. Questioned by the King about their actions, they claim not to see that they have done anything wrong. There begins a session of the parliament; however it is quickly interrupted by the unexpected arrival of John the Common-weill, representing the common people of Scotland. He seeks an audience with the King and Divyne Correctioun, and when it is granted, he explains the ways in which the Three Estates have 'gone backward' – they have been led by vice and oppressed the public. Divyne Correctioun calls on sergeants to arrest the vices Flatterie, Falset and Dissait, and they are put into the stocks.

[2498–2519]: Divyne Correctioun's attention then turns to Sensualitie and her attendants. Spiritualitie comes to Sensualitie's defence, assuring her that he will complain to the Pope about her treatment; however, Covetice takes his leave from the clergy, promising to return to their presence soon, and Sensualitie also makes a reluctant farewell to the representatives of the church.

[2520–2721]: Attention then turns to the temporal Estates, the nobles and merchants. John the Common-weill, Gude Counsall and the Pauper (who appeared in the interlude) set out the ills that have beset the nation, culminating in John the Common-weill's extended complaint against thieves, traitors, idlers, friars who do not attend to the spiritual needs of their flock, and corrupt judges who take bribes from criminals while punishing the poor. Divyne Correctioun acknowledges the merit of John's complaint and vows to reform the law. The noble Temporalitie agrees to reform if Spiritualitie also agrees; however, the senior representative of the church refutes John the Common-weill's charges, and claims exemption from punishment. The representatives of the temporal Estates then agree to repent, and Correctioun pardons them, so long as they vow to support the common people in the future.

[2722–2804]: Correctioun then asks John the Common-weill if he has any further complaint to make against the church, the third Estate. He declines, for fear, but Correctioun encourages him to speak, whereupon he and the Pauper expose the injustices of the church's imposition of death duties on poor cottagers. They complain that the church grows rich by imposing cruel taxes on the poor, a charge vehemently rejected by the representatives of Spiritualitie, who accuse John and the Pauper of heresy.

[2805–3004]: Gude Counsall halts the argument and asks the Estates to indicate their proposals for reform. The Merchants propose a land reform that will benefit labourers; however, Spiritualitie continues to refuse to agree to abolish the death duty. The other two temporal Estates outvote Spiritualitie and agree to write to the Pope, seeking the abolition of the tax. John the Common-weill then raises the issue of the burden of tax that is raised by the church in Rome, which threatens to bankrupt the nation. The Merchants observe that it is unjust that they, too, are taxed heavily so that churchmen can enjoy themselves in Rome. Gude Counsall acknowledges that it is now common for priests to run to Rome to buy benefices, that is, lucrative religious positions back home. He advises the Estates to support a reform that would mean that priests would deserve their official position, and that each priest could hold only a single office. Furthermore, he advises the Estates to ensure that bishops are able to do the job they are meant to do, namely preaching and attending to the moral education of the people. The representatives of Spiritualitie again respond angrily to these proposals and argue bitterly with Gude Counsall, the other Estates, the Pauper and John the Common-weill about the duties expected of them. This episode comes to a climax with an Abbess once again attempting to silence John the Common-weill by accusing him of heresy and Spiritualitie demanding that he be examined and then burned at the stake.

[3005–3065]: The vice, Flatterie, who is still in the disguise of Devotioun, a religious clerk, answers the call to examine John the Common-weill, and he challenges John to affirm his faith. After an angry exchange between John and Flatterie, Divyne Correctioun also demands that John state his beliefs. Thus prompted, he affirms his belief in the standard precepts of the church by reciting the Apostle's Creed. Correctioun demands that he expand on his beliefs, at which point John re-affirms his faith in the holy church, but not in its corrupt bishops and friars. Correctioun and the representatives of the two temporal Estates, led by the nobility, now side with John, and state their intention to ensure that in future those in religious office have the ability to discharge their spiritual duties. They instruct this intention to be noted down by a

Scribe, who complains that he has been writing all day without reward.

[3066–3115]: The Pauper now speaks out again, reminding the parliament to reform the consistorie, which was a type of court presided over by a bishop or his representative. Challenged by a parson, the Pauper complains that such courts use a legal jargon to confuse and oppress poor people, who are powerless to gain restitution. The representative of Temporalitie agrees that consistory courts should be reformed, as has been done in France, and that the Estate of Spiritualitie should have jurisdiction only over spiritual matters, while the two temporal Estates should pass laws only on secular matters. The representative of Spiritualitie objects strenuously to this proposal, but again the other two Estates overrule him.

[3116–3193]: The virtues, Veritie and Chastitite, then step forward to ask that justice be served on Spiritualitie for their wrongful imprisonment. Veritie claims that some poor craftsmen are more virtuous than bishops, and calls forward a craftsman to be examined to prove her case. The Taylour and Sowtar step forward and demonstrate that they are experts in their own trade. Correctioun marvels that poor tradesmen are masters of their craft, while wealthy religious men are ignorant of the duties of their office. He sends Diligence to the towns, cities and universities of the country to seek out and fetch educated churchmen who can indeed teach and preach.

[3194–3333]: The representative of Temporalitie then complains that the secular Estates cannot marry off their daughters without paying a tax to Spiritualitie, whose members marry off their own daughters to noble men with a rich dowry, and so increase their own property. Correctioun promises reformation in this matter, too. The mood abruptly changes as Common Thift enters, evidently escaping from some pursuer in the audience, and seeking a swift horse to return home to his mother. He spies the vice, Oppressioun, in the stocks, and asks him what he is doing there. Oppressioun tells Thift that he has only been imprisoned temporarily, and

A Satire of the Three Estates

asks him to take his place for a while; Thift agrees, they exchange places. Oppressioun then admits that he intends to leave him there and steal away from Fife forever.

[3334–3469]: Diligence returns with three learned religious clerks, including a Doctor of Divinity. King Humanitie, Divyne Correctioun and Gude Counsall instruct them to examine the representatives of Spiritualitie, to ensure that they can carry out their religious duties, and deprive those who cannot of their posts. Correctioun calls a representative of Spiritualitie to be thus examined. The representative shamelessly tells how he has increased his wealth by imposing various taxes, enjoyed four of five concubines, made his sons wealthy and married off his daughters to noble husbands. He bribes other lords to support him, in right and in wrong. Questioned about his competence in preaching, he states that he employs a friar to do that for him.

Chastitie then accuses an abbot and prioress of feigning abstinence and holiness while indulging in sexual excess. A scribe examines the Abbot, Persoun (Parson) and Priores, who admit, in turn, to drinking, having children through numerous affairs, providing richly for their children, playing boisterous games and gambling, and generally rejecting a virtuous life. Veritie calls upon Correctioun to demonstrate that some religious men can preach, and Correctioun instructs the Doctour to give a sermon.

[3469–3586]: The Doctour agrees, and, going to a pulpit, preaches a sermon on redemption as it is guaranteed by the passion of Christ and his sacrifice for fallen humanity. He focuses on the two commandments of the New Testament: to love God and to love one's neighbour as oneself. He concludes by exhorting his congregation to shun the sins of pride, envy, anger, lechery, jealousy, sloth and gluttony and to show charity and mercy to their fellows. The parson and abbot condemn the sermon as untruthful and unrealistic; the parson claims that pride is honesty, greed is wisdom, anger and gluttony are the food of life, and lechery is a natural indication of true love. Challenged by the Doctour, the parson points out that if these vices were sinful, men of the church would shun them. The Doctour responds by praying that God will reveal to the parson His truth.

[3587–3734]: At this point Diligence spies Flatterie, still disguised as a friar. He alerts the Doctour's learned companions to the fact that Flatterie intends to rouse up the town against them, at the instigation of Spiritualitie. The Doctour's companions question whether the town would rise against the lawful parliament, and Diligence points to the precedent of the Pope going to war against the king of France to defend the church's property. The learned churchmen observe that Christ himself owned no land, unlike his spiritual successors in the church. Diligence is astonished to learn of this fact, and asks why Veritie has been so badly treated by the church. The learned churchmen reply that the friars rely for their livelihood on their superiors' neglect of their duties; if those in higher office discharged these duties well, the friars would go unheeded. One clergyman urges the lords to reform the representatives of the church, and points to the Priores as unfit to carry out the work of Christ. At this exhortation, Divyne Correctioun commands two Sergeants to arrest and banish the friar and the prioress. The friar protests that he is above the law; however, the Sergeants take him and disrobe him, revealing him to be the vice, Flatterie. The Sergeant then causes the Priores to take off her nun's habit, revealing a rich silk dress underneath. The Priores renounces the life of the cloister, which she says her friends and companions forced her into, and goes to the town to become an alewife and seek an honest husband. Attention then turns to Flatterie, who agrees to help the parliament convict his fellow vices, Dissait and Falset, if he is spared his own life. He is sent to the gallows, where he confesses to his fellows that he has agreed to help hang them, and that all friars and nuns in the region are to be dispensed with, since they are against the interests of the common people.

[3735–3822]: Divyne Correctioun and King Humanitie, alongside the temporal Estates, then divest the still-protest-

A Satire of the Three Estates

ing representatives of the spiritual Estate of their elegant robes, and transfer them to the Doctour and his learned companions. The representatives of Spiritualitie seek out Dame Sensualitie and ask for her favour, but she and her attendant vices pretend not to know them. Spiritualitie, the Abbot and Persone depart, complaining. Gude Counsall and Divyne Correctioun then clothe John the Common-weill in bright and gorgeous clothes and ask him to take his place in the parliament.

[3823–3981]: Diligence then announces fifteen Acts of Parliament that the Three Estates have agreed in order to accomplish reformation. The Acts reaffirm the role of King Humanitie and the parliament in defending the Church of Christ and the rights of the common man. The Acts ensure the implementation of the law throughout Scotland, by establishing a second college of justice in the north; the parliament abolishes convents as unnecessary for religion, and resolves that their revenues be diverted to finance the two courts. The Parliament reaffirms that henceforth secular matters should be heard in secular courts and that religious (or consistory) courts should be confined to dealing with spiritual matters. Other Acts are concerned with ensuring that preachers are properly educated in the scriptures and that they hold no more than one religious office. Furthermore, the Scottish clergy are prevented from bankrupting poor people by imposing death duties, and from sending money to Rome except to support great Archbishoprics. Finally, priests are given licence to marry; however, the Parliament stipulates that each Estate should marry within its own bounds – the social order depends on the separation of spirituality and the nobility.

[3982–4271]: A Pauper then enters and congratulates the Estates on making such good laws; he then demands that Flatterie be banished and his fellow vices executed. Correctioun agrees, and the Sergeants carry out his order. Thift is brought before the gallows, where he makes a speech, calling for the repentance of all his fellow oppressors and transgres-

sors, and bidding farewell to all the craftsmen who aided him
in his misdoings. After he is hanged, Dissait is called forth.
He makes a similar speech, this time naming the merchants
who have conspired with him to trick their customers. He too
is hanged. Now it is Falset's turn: he also laments his situ-
ation, at length, and asks the craftsmen present how they
will thrive without him. He looks up at Commoun Thift and
Dissait, hanging on the gallows, and, as the cord is put round
his neck, makes a further speech, addressing a range of cov-
etous, corrupt, cruel and lustful people, and inviting them
to follow him to hell. As he is drawn up onto the gallows, a
black crow or jackdaw, representing his soul, is released.

[4272–4673]: Flatterie then congratulates himself on escaping the gallows and on having put a spell on the Three
Estates. He departs the stage, vowing to become a servant
to a learned Hermit and teach him how to flatter. At this
point Foly, a fool, enters and engages in banter with Diligence. King Humanitie calls him forward, and Foly complains to Humanitie and Correctioun, first about a sow that
has attacked him, and then about his violently flatulent wife.
He refuses Diligence's request to buy a couple of his fool's
bonnets; he then calls his children onstage to have lunch. Diligence upbraids him, and commands that he go to the King,
but Foly again refuses to obey. Diligence at length forces
him into the King's company. Foly asks what a pulpit is
doing in the King's presence. Diligence answers that it was
recently the site of a Bishop's sermon, at which Foly expresses
astonishment that a Bishop might preach, and asks what is to
become of poor friars. He then asks if the King will make
him a bishop, and King Humanitie responds by asking him
to give a sermon, commenting to his companions that Foly's
ravings will pass the time. Diligence responds that Foly
would be better suited to kitchen chores; however, he invites
him to speak, and Foly gives a mock sermon. Foly's sermon
demonstrates the extent to which folly characterises the material world: it causes some men to hoard gold only for others
to steal and spend; it causes merchants to risk bankruptcy
and death for ever-increasing profits; and it causes old and

A Satire of the Three Estates

impotent men to marry young girls who will be unfaithful to them. Diligence asks Foly whose hood he is holding; Foly responds that the hood is reserved for religious fools who seek holy office only to gain worldly wealth. He hesitates to speak further for fear of accusations of heresy; however, King Humanitie assures him that he is free to speak of anyone. Foly then claims that all present are fools, including kings who are willing to wage war and shed innocent blood for the sake of their own pride and lust for glory. His sermon ends with a garbled prophecy in cod Latin, much to Diligence's disgust. After a brief coda in which Foly asks the audience to pray for the soul of several notorious fools, Diligence calls the play to an end, asking the audience's indulgence, expressing his desire that the players have cheered their spirits, and instructing the minstrels to strike up a dance while he makes his way, urgently, to the tavern for a drink. Before he finally exits, he blesses the audience.

Activity
Estimates of the running time of the 1552 version of the play vary from between four and nine hours, depending on the number of intervals, and the manner of staging, etc. Modern productions vary from a 25-minute extract to a three hour performance. In short, many scenes have to be lost from the 1552 play-text. The episodic nature of the play allows modern editors and theatre directors to re-cut it in different ways – but each editorial and directorial decision changes the emphasis of the play – it is funnier or not so funny; more or less political; more or less obscene.

Look at the episodes listed above and decide what you would keep and which ones you would cut for a full, coherent performance of about two and a half to three hours (ie roughly 2500 lines of the 4673 lines of the 1552 text). You will need to cut around 2173 lines, nearly half of the 1552 text!

When you have made your decisions and considered their implications, look at Section 10 below on modern versions and productions of the play.

6. HISTORICAL AND POLITICAL BACKGROUND

By 1540, the year of the performance of the earliest known version of *Ane Satyre of the Thrie Estaitis,* Scotland was in the grip of a religious and political storm that had raged through all of the European continent. The Protestant Reformation had challenged the long-established power of the Catholic Church, and led to war in many European countries. England had become Protestant in 1534, in the reign of Henry VIII. After the English Reformation, friendly diplomatic relationships between Scotland and England were considered by some to be an implicit attack on Catholicism in Scotland. This religious and political unease is certainly the reason why we have a written description of the Twelfth Night performance of *Ane Satyre of the Thrie Estaitis* in 1540, whilst we lack detailed records of the many other performances of court entertainments. The political and religious content of this play – and the Scottish monarch's response to it – was of deep interest to the court in England. It was a Scottish Protestant with pro-English sympathies who made it his business to record a detailed description of the play and the king's immediate reaction:

> the King of Scottis Dide call vpon the busshope of Glascoe being Chancelour and diuerse other busshops / exorting thaym to reform thair facions and maners of lyving/ saying that oneles thay soe did / he wold send sex of the proudeste of thaym vnto his vncle of england...
>
> *the King of Scots did call upon the Bishop of Glasgow, being Chancellor, and diverse other bishops, exhorting them to reform their fashions and manners of living, saying that unless they so did, he would send six of the proudest of them to his English uncle [i.e. Henry VIII].*

Despite the apparent sympathy for reform inspired in the King by the performance of the play in 1540, relationships between Scotland and England deteriorated, and the two

A Satire of the Three Estates

nations went to war in 1542. This campaign was disastrous for the Scots, resulting in the James V's death from wounds received at the Battle of Solway Moss. By this time, Lyndsay was a prominent civil servant, the king's chief herald, known as the 'Lord Lyon King of Arms'. As noted earlier, he found himself with the sad task of being in charge of organising his former companion's funeral. James' daughter, Mary (who was later to become Queen of Scots), was still an infant, so Scotland was again ruled by governors, who often found themselves in conflict with Mary of Guise, James V's widow.

In the following years, the forces of religious reform in Scotland grew stronger, and bitter fighting between the Catholic and Protestant parties intensified. Decades of relatively stable government and peaceful prosperity that had characterised the reigns of James IV and James V slid inexorably into uncertainty and chaos. Scotland became torn between Protestants supported by allies in England and Catholics supported by allies in France. Nobles and churchmen took sides, some on the grounds of conscience, others to pursue their personal ambitions. The history of the period between James V's death in 1542 and the performance of the full version of *Ane Satyre of the Thrie Estaitis* in 1552 is characterised by atrocities ranging from the execution and murder of prominent churchmen on both sides of the Catholic-Protestant divide to violent clashes that saw the destruction of monasteries, abbeys and villages. Between 1544 and 1547, whole towns, including the city of Edinburgh, were set ablaze as a result of a series of attacks by English soldiers, a campaign known later as 'the Rough Wooing', a reference to Henry VIII's desire that James' infant daughter, Mary, should be contracted in marriage to his own son, Prince Edward. Eventually, James Hamilton, Earl of Arran and Scotland's first governor after the death of James V, successfully sought peace with England, and a measure of calm was temporarily restored to the nation.

The 1552 version of *Ane Satyre of the Thrie Estaitis* was therefore composed at a time when Lyndsay could easily have been looking back with longing to an earlier stage in his life, when he had enjoyed the role of companion and adviser to a youthful king. We can think of him revisiting and fleshing out a sketch or 'interlude' composed in happier days. The play is both a progressive and conservative response to current events by a complex playwright who could not be easily categorised as a sympathiser with only the Catholic or Protestant side in a bitter conflict, intensified by powerful agents in Protestant England and Catholic France.

Lyndsay's conservatism is evident in his explicit acceptance, despite its evident injustices, of the social order that the Three Estates represents. In medieval and renaissance Europe, society was seen as a rigid hierarchy. This feudal model of society emerged in France, and was exported to England at the time of the Norman Conquest in the 11th century. From England, it spread to lowland Scotland during the reign of King David I in the 12th century. By Lyndsay's time, this kind of society must have seemed natural, or even divinely approved. At the top of the social scale was the monarch; underneath him, as we have seen, were the Three Estates. The nobility consisted of the land-owning lords, who pledged allegiance to the monarch, and collected taxes from the common people who worked their land. The merchant classes, based in the burghs, enjoyed trading privileges granted by royal charter. They owed their living to the craftsmen who made the goods they bought and sold. The Catholic clergy had their own hierarchy, from bishop to humble priest, and they owed their privileges (and some of their income) to Rome as much as to the national monarch. The 'common people' were the peasants and their wives who worked the land and the craftsmen and women who produced the goods for merchants to sell.

Lyndsay does not question this model of society, nor does he seek to replace it. Rather, his social reforms are designed to strengthen the social hierarchy and make it even more rigid. The new laws proposed in lines 3823–3981 are designed to separate church and state, and also to police the boundaries within which members of social ranks can operate. Although priests will be allowed to marry, they (like other members of the community) will only be allowed to marry someone of their own social status. What Lyndsay is proposing is not unlike a caste system, whereby social groups are defined according to their spiritual or secular occupations, and mobility across the social groups is morally and legally discouraged.

A problem for most modern performances of the play is the substantial section (lines 3823–3981) in which Diligence announces no fewer than fifteen Acts of Parliament approved by the Three Estates to further social reform. These Acts target specific issues that Lyndsay feels need to be addressed for Scotland to become a fairer and more harmonious society. While many of these were urgent issues in the 16th century, and many of the audience would have had strong feelings about them, not all of them are as relevant today, and so they are difficult to dramatise. To take only a few examples from the list, Lyndsay calls for the establishment of a second College of Justice in Aberdeen. The first College of Justice, in Edinburgh, was a relative innovation. It had been established by James V in 1541, less than a year before the Twelfth Night performance of the earliest known version of *Ane Satyre of the Thrie Estaitis,* and it had come at the end of a long process during which the Crown had to persuade the church to subsidise a stronger and fairer system of justice in Scotland, in return for a promise of loyalty to Rome. Lyndsay in *Ane Satyre* is seeking to extend the new legal system to parts of Scotland that were more remote from the capital. Other Acts enforce the separation of church and state in matters of law, and demand that the taxes imposed by the church and sent to Rome are returned to Scotland in the form of support for major ecclesiastic institutions, such as the Archbishoprics of St Andrews or Aberdeen. A modern parallel might be that some of the money collected in Scotland to subsidise the European Union should be returned to Scotland through European support for particular projects.

Substantial parts of the second half of the play require some historical knowledge on the part of the reader, and, as already noted, anxious editors and directors tend to cut the sections that demand more specialist knowledge. It is also possible that the spectacle of the king's herald, Diligence, announcing parliamentary acts, even in the forum of live theatre, would be of compelling interest for the townsfolk of Cupar, at a time when there was little direct access to public life through any form of media. Today, saturated as we are by television and press coverage of public events and parliamentary proceedings, the spectacle of a herald announcing laws is less compulsive viewing. What modern spectators still value is the dramatic clash between social classes – the eruption of John the Common-weill and the Pauper into the dignified assembly of the great and the good, to complain of their oppression, to shame their so-called betters, and in so doing to change their world.

The main question that the play raises, historically and politically, is whether Lyndsay ultimately sides with the Catholic or Protestant factions that were dividing Scotland during his day. There is, as has been noted, evidence for both readings. Lyndsay, a good courtier, tends to side with the national monarch over the Pope in Rome – at least insofar as taxes raised in Scotland should be channelled back to Scotland in the form of support for the Scottish Archbishoprics. And certainly it will be clear by now that the church is the target for by far the most biting and extensive satire in *Ane Satyre of the Thrie Estaitis*. The reforms to the Catholic church that Lyndsay proposes are radical, and several – such as allowing priests to marry, and banning nuns – would not be countenanced by Catholicism, even half a millennium after the play was performed. However, the adoption of Catholic reforms does not make Lyndsay a Protestant, and both King Humanitie (once redeemed) and John the Common-weill leave the audience in no doubt that their adherence to what they regard as the true church of Christ is unwavering (see, for example, lines 3005–3065). In the final analysis, Lyndsay is suspicious of human institutions, secular and religious, for he knows that humanity is susceptible to folly, and therefore all institutions are corruptible. He understands that no matter whether the ruling party is Catholic or Protestant, Divyne Correctioun will always be required, sooner or later.

Activity

Look again at the timeline you have drawn of political events in Scotland from 1480–1560 (see Section 2 above). Using historical reference materials, from a library or from the web, draw another timeline of the Reformation from 1517–1598, as it particularly affected England, France and Scotland. The timeline should include the publication of Martin Luther's 95 theses; Henry VIII's declaration that the king was the head of the Church of England; the publication of the Book of Common Prayer in England; the publication of the Geneva Bible; the establishment of the Presbyterian Church of Scotland; the Council of Trent; the French Wars of Religion. When you have finished, look at the inter-relationship of the events, and in particular the influence in Scotland and France of members of the House of Guise. (Again, a sample chronology is given at the end of this Scotnote.)

7. LITERARY INFLUENCES ON THE PLAY

Part of understanding a literary work is understanding how it stands in relation to those works that precede and succeed it – how it fits into and helps shape a tradition. Unfortunately, we have no direct evidence of the influences that Lyndsay drew upon when writing *Ane Satyre of the Thrie Estaitis,* so we must rely upon indirect evidence and informed guesswork. We know from earlier sections that it is unlikely that Lyndsay went to university, and so he would not have had the opportunity to read plays or watch dramatic performances there – the universities, like the court, were a centre of dramatic production in the late middle ages and the renaissance period. However, it is likely that from a relatively young age he was involved in court performances: first as a spectator, then an actor, and later as a writer and director of court celebrations. No early theatrical performances, as such, survive in Scotland, but a flavour of them can be gained from reading the poetry of William Dunbar, much of which must have been performed at court when Lyndsay was a young man. Dunbar's poetry extends from a dignified, celebratory poem to mark the marriage of James IV to the English princess, Margaret Tudor, in 1503, to a farcical quarrel between two peasant lovers, 'In secreit place this hyndir nicht'. In 'The Lament for the Makaris', Dunbar names many writers whose work is lost to us now, intriguingly mentioning authors of 'tragedies'. Lyndsay shares with the elder poet the courtly taste for both pageantry and farce, and both are woven into *Ane Satyre*.

During his early years on his father's estate in the countryside, and probably even later, Lyndsay would also have witnessed players performing in the folk tradition. The earliest Scottish records of dramatic performance date from the 13th century, when church authorities tried to stop pagan seasonal rituals and fertility rites being performed in church grounds. One of these dramas, 'Plough Play' survives in a text of 1500, during Lyndsay's lifetime. Indeed, many references to Scottish folk drama in the 15th and 16th century are to May celebrations involving a mock king or queen (or a mock abbott), who leads the players in sketches, speeches, dancing and song, to musical accompaniment. Later, the 'King of the May', or the 'Abbot of Unreason', was succeeded by the popular figure of Robin Hood, imported from English tradition. It is likely that many of Lyndsay's audience in Cupar had watched May celebrations, and would have responded to parts of *Ane Satyre* as a sophisticated version of these irreverent forms of public entertainment. Indeed, they were so popular that in 1555, only three years after *Ane Satyre of the Thrie Estaitis* had presented its own mock king, abbots and abbesses in Cupar, they were suppressed by an act of parliament that threatened performers with fines and even banishment.

Lyndsay's years as guardian to the king seem to have allowed him time to read and develop his literary talent; his years as an ambassador to England and France will have certainly afforded him the opportunity to watch public celebrations in foreign courts, and no doubt he was also able to view dramatic performances, on the streets, in fields, or in theatres or spaces designated for performance, in and around Paris and London too. And, as we have already seen, other types of spectacle informed Lyndsay's playwriting – he understood the dramatic potential of public acts such as sermons, parliamentary debates, the announcement of new laws, and even the hanging of convicted criminals. Certainly, the rich diversity of the episodes in *Ane Satyre of the Thrie Estaitis* shows that Lyndsay was able to make a new dramatic work, with particularly Scottish themes, from a whole range of sources that had their origins within and far beyond the boundaries of the nation. In this brief space, we can only look in detail at a few. The overall structure of the play has been shown to entwine together three different dramatic traditions: morality play – farce – *sottie* (a comic tradition that demonstrates that the world is ruled by Folly). We shall consider each of these in turn.

The first half of *Ane Satyre of the Thrie Estaitis* follows the general pattern of a morality play – indeed, one modern edition of the play includes it with three English examples of this form, some of which might have been known to Lyndsay, *King Johan, Magnyficence,* and *The Castle of Perseverance.* Morality plays are related to mystery plays, which were popular performances that spread knowledge of scenes from the Old and New Testaments. Despite their religious content, mystery plays cover a range of styles, from the comic bawdiness of a drunken and half-naked Noah, to the agonies of the Crucifixion and the triumph of the Resurrection. Morality plays also served to dramatise religious teachings. However, morality plays, or *interludes*, as they are sometimes known, dramatise the spiritual journey of an individual, often an Everyman figure. The plot of the morality play usually concerns an individual who succumbs to temptation, endures the pain of despair, is redeemed by God's grace, and whose soul achieves salvation. The story of this representative individual is usually told through an extended metaphor or *allegory* – and so the plot of salvation can be told as if it were a journey, or a battle. In *Ane Satyre of the Thrie Estaitis,* the fall of King Humanitie is dramatised as the seduction of a young and inexperienced man by a worldly courtesan, Dame Sensualitie. The operation of grace and redemption is presented as the arrival of an ambassador, an emissary sent directly by God to banish vice and re-establish harmony through the enactment of divine law. Lyndsay may well have seen English morality plays when he was on diplomatic missions to the court in London; while he adapts and shapes the form to his own devices, making the morality tale only the backbone of the first half of his play, he does adopt some of the conventions of this tradition, notably in allowing the chief vices, Sensualitie and Flatterie, to escape.

The second tradition that Lyndsay draws upon is that of the farce. Farces are less obviously didactic than morality plays – that is, they are intended less to teach and more simply to entertain. Farces are associated not so much with vices and virtues as with stock characters in comic conflict to no discernible moral purpose. Incompatible husbands and wives are a recurrent theme, and they re-occur in *Ane Satyre of the Three Estaitis* in several scenes. For example, the Cupar Banns have an Auld Man who fails to restrain the promiscuity of his amorous young wife, Bessie, and the Cottar, Sowtar and Taylour all have shrill, shrewish wives whose only pleasure seems to be in giving them grief. In his introduction

A Satire of the Three Estates

and notes to the Canongate edition, Professor Lyall suggests that a French play, *La Farce d'un Pardonneur,* is a possible source of the episode of the Sowtar's divorce from his wife, in the interlude (lines 2087–2186). As we have seen earlier, this episode causes problems for some modern editors and directors, who cut it from their adaptations or performances. The combination of high-minded morality play and irreverent, bawdy farce is a difficult one for some modern readers and performers, since it suggests an inconsistency of style and artistic purposes. One aspect of the play that it is important to consider is its adherence to an aesthetic that allows the portrayal of the most serious matters to be undercut by riotous, comic and downright rude episodes.

Professor Lyall's introduction to the Canongate edition also gives valuable background to the third main pillar in the structure of *Ane Satyre of the Thrie Estaitis,* namely the French *sottie* plays, in which one character plays the Fool, in an appropriate costume, and the comedy is based on the assumption that folly, rather than wisdom, governs the world. The irreverent inversion of conventional values represented by the *sottie* tradition is similar in some respects to that of May plays in which the moral order is also turned upside-down by the Abbot of Unreason. The Fool, or Foly, appears twice in *Ane Satyre of the Thrie Estaitis,* in the Cupar Banns to frighten the farcical character of the cowardly, boastful soldier, and again at the end of Part Two, to preach a parody of the learned Doctour's sermon (lines 4502–4673). Here the influence of the *sottie* is at its strongest in Lyndsay's play, as Foly effectively casts a sceptical eye over the reforms enacted by the learned reformers, and reminds everyone of the foolishness ingrained in the world, from the highest to the lowest in rank (lines 4585–6):

Conforming to my first narratioun
Ye ar all fuillis, be Cokis passioun!

The character of Foly, introduced so close to the end of the play, and so shortly after the exit of Flatterie, has prompted some modern adapters and directors of the play to conflate the two characters into one. This decision has some interesting consequences, since the character of Flatterie shares some of the attributes of Foly, and he certainly makes fools of others; however, there is a case for keeping them separate, since Flatterie is an active participant in the vicious oppression of the kingdom, whereas Foly is closer to a 'wise fool' whose role at the close of proceedings is to cast a comically sceptical and withering eye on the hopes and pretensions of the parliament of the Three Estates.

Activity

To explore further the literary influences on *Ane Satyre of the Thrie Estaitis*, you will need to be prepared to hunt down and read some further texts. Peter Happé's *Four Morality Plays* (Penguin, 1979) and Greg Walker's *Medieval Drama: An Anthology* (Blackwell, 2000) both include *Ane Satyre* amongst a variety of English morality and miracle plays. Happé's anthology allows comparison of Lyndsay's play with three English examples that predate or were written around the same time as the Scottish author's work – *The Castle of Perseverance* (Anonymous, 1400–1425), *Magnyfycence* (John Skelton, 1515–18), *King Johan* (John Bale, 1538–60). Of the three, *Magnyfycence* is a good place to start, since Skelton also takes a prince as his hero, and possibly bases him loosely on Henry VIII, just as Lyndsay's portrait may owe something to James V. Skelton's play, however, is less immediately political than Lyndsay's and is more concerned to illustrate the general moral that a ruler must use measured restraint in his use of the wealth at his command – if he is reckless, and listens to deceitful and self-serving advice, then he loses his wealth and he and his kingdom suffer. His redemption comes with the arrival of Good Hope. It is illuminating to compare key characters in each play, e.g. Rex Humanitas and Magnyfycence; Flatterie and Counterfet Countenaunce; Divyne Correctioun and Good Hope; and, of course, Foly in each play. For example, Good Hope describes himself as a spiritual apothecary, or doctor, and he promises to relieve Magnyfycence's suffering with his medicine (lines 2350–6):

Good Hope, your potecary assygned am I,
That Goddes Grace hath vexed you sharply,
And payned you with a purgacyon of odyous Poverte,
Myxed with bytter alowes of herde Adversyte. *a purgative*
Nowe must I make you a lectuary softe,   *sweet medicine*
I to mynyster it, you to recyve it ofte,
With rubarbe of repentaunce in you for to rest...

Lyndsay's Divyne Correctioun is altogether sterner (lines 1621–2)

> I am ane judge, richt potent and seveir,
> Come to do justice mony thowsand myle.

By comparing Lyndsay's play with earlier examples of the different dramatic sources he draws on, we can more easily see what makes *Ane Satyre of the Thrie Estaitis* an original and distinctive drama.

8. STAGING THE PLAY IN THE 16TH CENTURY

A survey of Lyndsay's literary influences prompts a brief consideration of the resources available to him to stage the play. Again, we have no detailed record of who the actors and actresses were, or how the play was staged in any of its known performances, in Linlithgow, Cupar or Edinburgh. Even the three performances that we know about are likely to have been quite different. The original version was a shorter 'interlude' performed in Linlithgow Palace on Twelfth Night in January, 1540. Although the Palace is now a ruin, it is still possible to visit this site and stand in the likely venue, the great hall on the east side. If the description of the play is reliable, there were about thirteen players, who would have acted on a stage erected for the purpose. Music might have been played from the minstrel's gallery. Props would have included a throne for the player-king. According to surviving treasurer's accounts, the production was an expensive one.

The second performance was a greatly extended version, presented in the open air on a playfield in Cupar in June, 1552. The playfield was bounded by a stream, the Lady Burn, which might have separated the players from the audience, and which was used as a natural 'prop' in the play. In lines 1375–95, for example, the Sowtar's and Taylour's wives exit by wading across the stream, which causes the Sowtar's Wyfe to complain (1388–91):

> Then help me for to kilt my clais.
> Quhat gif the paddoks nip my tais?
> I dreid to droun heir, be Sanct Blais   1390
>   Without I get support.

[Then help me to kilt up my clothes./What if the frogs nip my toes?/I'm afraid I'll drown here, by St Blais/ Unless I get some help.]

It has been suggested that the audience sat above the playfield on Castle Hill in Cupar, and looked down on the acting area, which would have included a throne, a pulpit and a scaffold. Rather than being an intimate court entertainment with thirteen players, it was now a public spectacle, with 43 roles to be played, and pageantry on a grand scale, as when the Three Estates enter walking backwards. Obviously there is scope for actors in more minor roles 'doubling' their parts, but the stage directions suggest that many of the actors who are not participating in the action at any one time remain seated within the audience's view.

The final performance took place in August, two years later, on another playfield, Greenside, below Calton Hill in Edinburgh, before Mary of Guise, James V's widow. By this time, Mary of Guise had assumed power and was governing Scotland as Queen Regent. She, it will be remembered, was present with her late husband at the original production in Linlithgow Palace. The third performance could well have been a revival of the extended Cupar version, but probably with the local references omitted. Charteris, the publisher of the play, records that it lasted from nine in the morning until six in the evening. Ground was cleared for the performance, and a special 'hous' was erected to protect the Queen Regent from the weather.

We have no record of who the actors were. From the example of Lyndsay himself, it is clear that talented courtiers were drafted into performances, as he was when in his early twenties. As noted earlier, there is the unsubstantiated but plausible tradition that he took the part of Diligence in his greatest work. Actors for the other parts might have been drawn from the social classes they represent. The popularity of folk festivities such as May festivals gave scope for common folk, of both sexes, to participate in public performance of different kinds. Certainly, in continental Europe and England it was known for the labouring classes to participate in drama. William Tydeman observes that in the Kentish Passion plays, which were dramas of scenes from the life of Christ, performed in New Romney in 1556 and 1560, an innkeeper, brewer, baker and butcher played key roles, while in Metz in the mid 15th century, a glazier's daughter played the role of St Catherine so movingly that she reduced spectators to tears and won a rich husband in marriage.

In between the social ranks of courtier and tradesman, certain professions – such as the law and even the church – allowed individuals with a talent for public speaking to show off their skills, and some of these might well have been tempted into dramatic performance, if the opportunity arose. It was not uncommon for clergymen to play roles in Passion plays, although it seems unlikely that churchmen would have been flocking to portray themselves as the villains in Lyndsay's satirical play. In addition, the 16th century saw an increasing professionalisation of the theatre, and it is likely that Lyndsay would have combined paid and unpaid players in all three performances of his play.

Activity

Take one episode from the play involving three or more players, and consider in detail how you would stage it. A possible example is the episode between the Pardoner, the Pauper and Wilkin in lines 2187–2300. Now imagine that you are giving instructions to a trio of amateur actors. What kind of physical space will the actors occupy, and how should they relate to each other and to the audience? Sketch out the performance area, and write detailed notes on the movements of the actors, when they should direct their dialogue to each other, when they should direct their dialogue to the audience, how else they might interact with the audience, and how they might use props to heighten their performance.

9. LANGUAGE AND STYLE

Perhaps the greatest challenge to modern readers and viewers of *Ane Satyre of the Thrie Estaitis* is the relative unfamiliarity of Lyndsay's 16th century Scots dialogue, particularly when it is seen on the page. Lyndsay's dramatic medium is a robust variety of Older Scots, from the end of what scholars refer to as the Early Middle Scots period (1450–1550). By the mid 16th century, the Scots language had long extended beyond speech to supplant Latin as the written medium of national and burgh law in Scotland, and French as the preferred language for literature. Lyndsay was therefore writing in what he would have considered the natural vehicle for literary expression, both high and low, in Scotland. However, given that he was a playwright we might expect some aspects of his dramatic verse to retain some features of everyday Scots speech.

Even so, it is well to remember that Lyndsay himself would not have thought of his own language as 'Scots'. Indeed, he refers to his fellow poet, Gavin Douglas, as 'of our Inglis [i.e. English] rethorick, the rose' in 'The Testament and Complaynt of Our Soverane Lordis Papyngo' (line 24). Lyndsay, like many of his contemporaries, ironically with the exception of Gavin Douglas, seemed to consider his own language and that of his southern neighbours as one and the same. Douglas seems to have been one of the few in his day to employ different labels for 'Scots' and 'English', most famously in the Preface to the first book of his translation of the *Aeneid*. While today we might follow Douglas and make much of the differences between Scots and English forms of writing and speech, it is equally possible to overstate the difficulties posed by Lyndsay's dramatic verse to readers schooled in modern English prose. With a little effort, it quickly becomes familiar and easier to comprehend.

Spelling
All modern editions 'normalise' the spelling of the Bannatyne manuscript and the original printed editions to some extent, printing older letters such as þ as *th* and ſ as *s*.

Even after the spelling has been normalised, the look of words on the page can still seem strange at first. Consider the following passage from a speech by Dame Sensualitie (lines 271–8):

Heir sall entir Dame Sensualitie with hir madynnis Hamelines and Denger.

SENSUALITIE: Luifars awalk! behald the fyrie spheir,
   Behauld the naturall dochter of Venus;
   Behauld, luifars, this lustie ladie cleir,
   The fresche fonteine of knichtis amorous,
   Repleit with joyis dulce and delicious.   275
   Or quha wald mak to Venus observance
   In my mirthfull chalmer melodious,
   Thair sall thay find all pastyme and pleasance.

While the language here might at first sight look difficult, if you read the passage aloud, you will quickly see that there are really only a few words – *dulce* (sweet) and *pleasance* (pleasure) – that are no longer used today. To familiarise yourself with the spellings it is best to take a few shorter passages like this and look for recurring patterns such as the following:

- *f* is sometimes used where we now expect to see *v*, as in 'luifars' (lovers)
- *au* is used in Scots where English has *o*, as in *behauld*, *auld* (behold, old)
- *ei* indicates an 'ee' sound, nowadays variously spelled, as in *heir* (here), *spheir* (sphere), *cleir* (clear) and *repleit* (replete). Note that *fonteine* (fountain) would have been pronounced in the same way.
- *l* before a consonant is often silent and simply changes the sound of the preceding vowel, as in *awalk* (awake) and *chalmer* (chamber)
- *quh* corresponds to *wh* as in *quha* (who)
- *s* or *sch(e)* can correspond to present-day *sh*, as in *sall* (shall) and *fresche* (fresh)

A Satire of the Three Estates

- *y* can be used for *i* as in *fyrie* (fiery), *pastyme* (pastime), and *satyre* (satire), and also for the short unstressed vowel in words like *madynnis* (maidens)
- *–ie* is used where we now expect *y,* as in *Sensualitie* (Sensuality), *fyrie* (fiery), *lustie* (lusty)

There are of course other differences, but the ones noted above are fairly common, and once attention has been drawn to them and a few others (such as the *–ioun* ending that is found in many Latinate terms, such as *commissioun, perditioun, narratioun,* and so on), the spelling of the text becomes much less impenetrable. By far the best strategy for familiarising yourself with Lyndsay's spelling is to read the play aloud.

Vocabulary and idiom

A more problematical issue is vocabulary and idiom. Many of Lyndsay's Scots terms have been lost to today's speech, and even some of the words that seem familiar had a different meaning and function in 16th century Scotland. Some of the problems can be seen in a passage such as the following exchange between Divyne Correctioun and John the Commonweill (lines 2724–2741):

> JOHNE: Na, sir, I dar nocht speik ane word
>   To plaint on preists, it is na bourd!   2725
> CORRECTIOUN: Flyt on thy fow fill, I desyre the,
>   Swa that thou schaw bot the veritie.
> JOHNE: Grandmerces, then I sall nocht spair
>   First to compleine on the Vickair:
>   The pure cottar being lyke to die,   2730
>   Haifand young infants twa or thrie,
>   And hes twa ky, bot ony ma,
>   The Vickar most haif ane of thay
>   With the gray frugge that covers the bed,
>   Howbeit the wyfe be purelie cled;   2735
>   And gif the wyfe die on the morne,
>   Thocht all the bairns sould be forlorne,

> The uther kow he cleiks away,
> With the pure cot of raploch gray.
> Wald God this custome war put doun   2740
> Quhilk never was foundit be ressoun!

Some of the spelling conventions noted above reappear here, and again it is helpful to read the passage aloud to try to understand the gist before looking at the vocabulary and idioms in detail. If you do so, you will probably understand that John the Common-weill has been invited to complain about the treatment that poor people have suffered at the hands of the clergy (*to plaint on priests*). He refuses at first, but when encouraged, tells a story about a poor farmer (*pure cottar*) and his wife and children *(young infants twa or thrie)*. If both the cottar and wife die, the priest (*the vickair*) takes their possessions as death duty. When the husband dies, he takes *ane of the twa ky* and *the gray frugge that covers the bed*. When the wife dies, he takes *the uther kow* and *the pure cot of raploch gray*. The priest does not care whether *all the bairnis sould be forlorne*. John is clearly vexed by this *custome*.

It is a good idea to try to work out the general sense of a passage before looking up a word in a glossary or dictionary. A glossary can then confirm your predictions that John fears that it is no joke (*bourd*) to complain (*flyt*) about priests, and that the priest is intent on taking the cottar's cattle (*ky*), blanket or quilt (*frugge*), or rough grey coat (*pure cot of raploch gray*).

Most good editions come with a glossary, either sharing the page with the dialogue or collected at the end. These can be used actively to enrich your Scots vocabulary; for example, you can begin a personal dictionary or topic-based 'thesaurus' of terms you like or find particularly useful, such as terms for animals (*kow*, *ky*), occupations (*cottar*, *vickair/preist*), or terms of complaint (*plaint*, *flyt*, *compleine*). When a word in the glossary looks particularly interesting, you can do further research on it, using the Dictionary of the Scots Language (DSL) online at **www.dsl.ac.uk**. The DSL gives a wonderfully rich history for many of the terms in Early Middle Scots, and shows how the term has been used in different

A Satire of the Three Estates

contexts. For example, looking up the term *raploch* in the DSL gives the following information:

> **RAPLOCH**, n., adj. Also rap(p)lach; raplack, raplock; rablogh; erron. ramploch.
> I. n. 1. Coarse homespun woollen cloth which is undyed (Sc. 1808 Jam.; Uls. 1953 Traynor); a garment made of this. Also raploch-grey, id.
>   *Sc. 1816 Scott O. Mortality xl.: *His douce raploch-grey, and his band wi' the narrow edging.*
>   *Sc. a.1854 D. Vedder Poems (1878) 348: *Ophelias in woollen raplochs, and Desdemonas in linsey woolsey frocks.*
>   *Uls. 1878 Trans. Hist. Soc. Lan. & Chs. XXX. 115: *As coarse as raploch.*
>   *Kcb. 1900: *The warp and weft of raploch are not driven closely together in the loom.*
>   *Sc. 1913 H. P. Cameron Imit. Christ I. xxv. 47: *Their scran is puir, their cleed in ramploch.*
>   [O.Sc. roploch, = I., 1., 1530, rapploch gray, 1540. Of obscure origin.]
>
> *Extract from DSL entry for raploch with selected citations.*

The dictionary entry shows that *raploch* and *raploch gray* are Older Scots terms, the earliest recordings of which are during Lyndsay's lifetime. The other citations show that the word has enjoyed an enduring literary life, appearing up until the 20th century in contexts referring to the roughly-spun clothing of poorer people. Indeed, the term becomes symbolic of a kind of coarse poverty.

Study of the language of *Ane Satyre of the Thrie Estaitis* can be enlivened by dictionary study of the history of certain key terms, and indeed the language of the play can stimulate an exploration of areas of early Scots life, such as the law.

Activity
Using the DSL online (**www.dsl.ac.uk**), look up some of the legal terms found in the discussion between

the Pauper, Temporalitie and Spiritualitie (lines 3072–3115): *consistorie, pleinye, defame, persew, conclude, failye, profeit singular, consent, disassent, instrument,* and so on.

Look at the definitions and the other citations. Then summarise what you have learnt about the Scottish legal system in Lyndsay's time.

Common vocabulary

Many of the vocabulary items in the play, of course, often recur, and it is useful taking some time to familiarise yourself with them. They are usually grammatical terms such as *but* (often meaning 'without' or 'except') and common verbs, such as *gang* ('go') and *haif* (have) Once these terms have been memorised, reading the play can become a more fluent and enjoyable experience. In his introduction to the Canongate edition, Professor Lyall provides a useful list of common vocabulary items, which can be turned into simple vocabulary learning activities for readers who are new to reading older forms of the language.

Activity

Look at Professor Lyall's list of common words in the play, reproduced below but without their meanings. Match the Older Scots words with the meanings shown below. Answers are given at the end of this book.

1. als	8. but	15. lufe	22. or	29. sic/sik
2. althocht	9. eine	16. luik	23. quha	30. sould
3. awin	10. fra	17. maist	24. quhair	31. sune
4. ay	11. gang	18. na	25. quhen	32. syne
5. baith	12. gif, give	19. nane	26. quhilk	33. thir
6. be	13. haif	20. nocht	27. quhill	34. till
7. beir	14. intill	21. nor	28. sen	35. yit

Meanings:

have	look	where	as, also
which	when	yet	to
from	then	most	such

no, nor, than	these	but, without	although
in, into	go	own	than
if	always, ever	until	carry
eyes	not	soon	love
both	none	should	since
be, by	or, before	who	

'Bad' language

There is, of course, a particular sense of 'language' that might trouble readers and audiences of this play – its occasional use of sexual obscenities and its frequent use of blasphemous expressions. The sexual language of the play is frank and sometimes used technically – one of the most offensive words in present-day English is used in the matter-of-fact context of a stage direction in the Cupar Banns. This is not to say that sexual language had less of an impact on 16th century audiences. A substantial proportion of the play depends on broad comedy, and explicit sexual insults such as *huirson* ('whoreson', 'son of a bitch') perhaps carried even more of an inflammatory charge in the 16th century than they do today. However, there is a greater variety and frequency of mildly blasphemous expressions, used by most of the characters and in many scenes, e.g.

Be God, I see him at the last (l. 134)
I rew richt sair, *be Sanct Michell* (l. 461)
Good morrow, Maister, *be the Mes*! (l. 475)
That will we nocht yet, *be Sanct Bryde* (l. 1092)
Remaine wee heir, *be God Him-sell* (l. 1520)
Now, weill said, *be the Sacrament*! (l. 1549)
Thou hes done weill, *be Godis mother*! (l. 2220)
Now, *be Him that herryit Hell* (l. 4307)

The examples show that many aspects of Christianity are drawn upon by the characters in their swearing: God, His mother, the holy sacrament, the mass, and various saints. The reference to 'Him that herryit Hell' refers to a popular medieval belief in the 'Harrowing of Hell', that is, an apocryphal episode in which Jesus is supposed to have descended into Hell in the three days between the Crucifixion and the

Resurrection in order to save the souls lost before his appearance on earth. The abundance of swearing in the play may have several functions. First, these expressions give the dialogue a pungent, colloquial flavour; secondly, the formulaic phrases usefully fill out the lines of verse, and often provide Lyndsay with a convenient rhyme; thirdly their religious quality may ironically underscore the spiritual themes explored more seriously by the play.

Aureate or 'golden' language

One of the enjoyable characteristics of the language of *Ane Satyre of the Thrie Estaitis* is the way it sweeps its audience from the low-life farcical episodes, to high parliamentary and religious performance, and back again. To raise the tone of the parliamentary and religious episodes, Lyndsay draws upon a linguistic resource that long had heightened the style of Scots poetry, namely a deep pool of vocabulary appropriated from Latin. Latin had once been the language of law, learning and the church. Medieval Scots poets, or 'makars', had referred to the *aureate* ('golden') nature of Latin, which until Lyndsay's time was still considered a language far superior to any of the European vernacular languages, like French or English.

Aureation itself has several forms. The technical Latinate language of the law and officialdom, which filters into Scots partly through French, echoes in the heraldic utterances of Diligence, as in lines 46–53 (Latinate terms are italicised):

> And heir be oppin *proclamatioun*
> I wairne in name of his *magnificence*
> The Thrie *Estaitis* of this *natioun*
> That they *compeir* with detfull *diligence*
> And till his *Grace* mak their *obedience*; 50
> And first I wairne the *Spiritualitie*,
> And sie the *burgesses* spair not for *expence*,
> Bot speid thame heir with *Temporalitie*.

The learned Latin of the church is evident in the sermon given by the Doctor, for example when he begins to preach about the way in which God created Adam ('our foir-father')

A Satire of the Three Estates

in his own likeness (or 'image'), and how God's innate (or 'ingent') love remained when he fell prey to the temptation of the Devil (lines 3483–3490):

> Tuiching nathing the great *prerogative*
> Quhilk God to man in his *creatioun* lent,
> How man of nocht creat *superlative*
> Was to the *image* of God *Omnipotent*,
> Let us *consider* that *speciall* luife *ingent*
> God had to man quhen our foir-father fell
> Drawing us all in his loynis *immanent*
> Captive from *gloir* in thirlage to the Hel...   3490

John the Common-weill can draw upon the linguistic resources of Latinate Scots when the occasion demands it, as in his commendation of the lords of Temporalitie (lines 2841–2845):

> My lords, ye haif richt *prudentlie concludit*.
> Tak tent now how the land is clein *denudit*
> Of gould and silver, quhilk daylie gais to Rome
> For buds, mair then the rest of Christendome.   2845

As the excerpts suggest, the quality and density of the Latinate Scots can vary according to the characterisation: Diligence comes across as officious, the Doctour as learned and John as plain-speaking. But aureate language is not simply legal and ecclesiastical. The makars raised the tone of their love poetry, too, and Dame Sensualitie's seductive eroticism also has Latin resonances, again often conveyed into Scots via French (e.g. lines 271–8):

> Luifers awalk! behald the fyrie *spheir*,
> Behald the *naturall* dochter of Venus;
> Behald, luifers, this lustie lady *cleir*,
> The fresche *fonteine* of knichtis *amorous*,
> *Repleit* with joyis *dulce* and *delicious*.   275
> Or quha wald mak to Venus *observance*
> In my mirthfull *chalmer melodious*,
> Thair sall thay find all pastyme and *pleasance*.

Lyndsay's use of Latinate terms to heighten or 'gild' his dramatic verse comes towards the end of a period of veneration of the classical tongue. Just as *Ane Satyre* was being performed in Scotland, in France the poet Joachim du Bellay was publishing *La Défence et illustration de la langue françoise* (1549). This pamphlet, while advocating a return to classical models for French poetry, declared that modern European languages had as much claim to literary respect as did Latin. Du Bellay's example was taken up by poets across Europe and a new nationalist pride in Scots vernacular language can be seen in the generations of Scottish poets towards the end of the 16th century. But for Lyndsay, as for his literary predecessors, and indeed some of his successors, Latinate language acted as a powerful stylistic marker in his verse, and it is worth paying attention to. Densely Latinate language was redolent of secular power, hard-won learning, religious mystery and even erotic promise.

Activity
Take a look at a relatively long speech (at least 15 lines each) by two of the characters, a virtuous character and one of the vices. Count the number of times that each character uses an obscene or mildly blasphemous expression (e.g. 'marry', a reference to the Virgin Mary) and each time that the character uses a long, Latinate word (e.g. 'omnipotent'). Are the distributions equal or unequal? How does the choice of vocabulary act as a signal of the nature of the characters in the play?

Grammar
The grammar of Lyndsay's Scots verse is similar, perhaps surprisingly similar, to the grammar of contemporary English, and only a few differences merit a mention. Once understood, these grammatical features should again make the language of the play a little easier to comprehend.

Grammar is about the form of individual words and how they combine. For example, the noun *king* has a plural form which, today, is made by adding an ending *–s*. The verb *want* has a present-tense form, also made by adding *–s,* and a past-tense form, made by adding *–ed*. Lyndsay's Scots is almost identical in principle, but slightly different in detail. To make a noun plural, Lyndsay added an *–s, –is* or *–es* ending. To indicate a present-tense verb, he also used an *–s* or *–is* ending, and to indicate a past-tense verb he used a *–t* or *–it* ending. These forms can be seen very frequently throughout the play, for example, in the exchange between Divyne Correctioun, King Humanitie and Dame Sensualitie (lines 1701–3; 1734–9):

> CORRECTIOUN: Get up, Sir King! Ye haif sleipit aneuch   *'sleeped'/slept*
> Into the armis of Ladie Sensual.   *arms*
> Be sure that mair belangis to the pleuch...   *belongs*
> SENSUALITIE: I care nocht that; als gude luif cums as gais.   *comes as goes*
> I recommend yow to the Queene of Farie;
> I se ye will be gydit with my fais.   *guided, foes*
> As for this king, I cure him nocht twa strais: *straws*
> War I amang bischops and cardinals   *bishops and cardinals*
> I wald get gould, silver and precious clais.   *clothes*

In one respect, however, the grammatical form of Lyndsay's verbs is slightly different from that found today. Today we have an *–ing* ending on both the verb when it is found in a full verb phrase (e.g. *is/was coming*) or as a non-finite verb without an auxiliary (*coming home, I found*...) We also add an *–ing* ending when we turn the verb into a noun or use it to describe a noun, as in *I dread his coming; the coming thing.* In Lyndsay's day, Scots might still distinguish between the use of such words in verb phrases and in noun phrases. When these words were used as verbs, older Scots speakers added the endings *–and, –an* or *–in*. Only when the word was turned into a noun did it have the ending *–ing*. These distinctions are less commonly found in *Ane Satyre of the Thrie Estaitis,* but they are there. Below we can see two examples of the verbal ending (lines 443, 3755) and two examples where verbs are turned into nouns (lines 387–8; 1585–6):

Pass ye befoir, and say I am cummand.   *coming*

With glorious habit rydand on your muillis   *riding*

And say I ly in languisching   *languishing*
Except scho mak remeid.

I will do nocht without the conveining   *convening*
Ane Parliament of the Estaitis all.

As the examples show, when the verb is used as a noun, it is often preceded by a preposition (*in, on, to,* etc), an article (*ane, the*) or a possessive adjective (*thy, my,* etc) However, by Lyndsay's time this grammatical distinction was being lost, and we can see an example where even Lyndsay mixes the *–and* and *–ing* forms up, as below, when he uses *–ing* to indicate a verb (lines 2534–5):

That sall I do within schort space
Praying the Lord to send us grace.

For the purpose of comprehension, readers need simply remember that Lyndsay often ends verbal forms with *–and* when today we would write *–ing,* as in lines 3589–90):

For be the counsall of yon flattrand freir   *flattering*
Thay purpois to mak all this toun on steir.

Activity
Look at a reasonably long speech by one or two of the characters. Read it carefully and mark each example of a word ending in –is, –it, –ing and –and. Now sort them under the following headings:
- Plural nouns
- Present-tense verbs
- Past-tense verbs
- –ing verbs

Rhyme and Metre

Ane Satyre of the Thrie Estaitis is written in a number of verse forms, which Lyndsay uses to suit the mood of the different episodes. Grand scenes featuring righteous or noble characters and their representatives are written in longer, pentameter lines – that is, each line potentially contains five stressed syllables, shown below in **bold**. In such episodes the lines often rhyme *abab*, as in Gude Counsall's address to King Humanitie (lines 554–9):

> Im**mor**tall **God, maist** of ma**gni**fi**cence**,
> Quhais **Majes**tie na **clark** can **compre**hend,   555
> Must **save** yow **all** that **giv**is sic **audience**
> And **grant** yow **grace Him nev**er till of**fend**,
> Quhilk **on** the **Croce** did **willinglie ascend**
> And **sched** His **pret**ious **blude** on **everie side**...

Scenes featuring the vices tend to be less grand, marked by shorter lines that allow for faster-paced comedy. Most of these lines potentially have four stressed syllables, again shown in bold below. The rhymes may be couplets (*aabbcc*) or a 'tail-rhyme' stanza form that was often used in comic poetry (*aabaab*). In the 'tail-rhyme' stanza the b-rhyme has only three stressed syllables, as in the following exchange between Dissait, Flatterie and Falset (lines 1515–20; 1546–51), in which they decide to steal the King's box of treasure before escaping Divyne Correctioun's judgement. Notice that in Dissait's dialogue with Falset, one vice completes the other's 'tail-rhyme' stanza:

> DISSAIT: **Broth**er, **heir** ye yon **pro**cla**ma**tioun?   1515
>   I **dreid** full **sair** of **reforma**tioun;
>   Yon **mess**age **maks** me **mang**it.
>   **Quhat** is your **counsell, to** me **tell**?
>   **Remaine** wee **heir**, be **God** Him-**sell**,
>   Wee **will** be **all** thre **hang**it.   1520
> [...]
> DISSAIT: **Fals**et, I **wald** wee **maid** ane **band**,
>   **Now**, quhill the **King** is **yit** sle**pand**.
>   Quhat **rak** to **steill** his **box**?

> FALSET: Now, **weill said**, be the **Sacra**ment!
> I **sall** it **steill** in**con**tinent,   1550
>   Thocht **it** had **twen**tie **lox**.

The eruption of John the Common-weill into the grand parliament of the Three Estates and his interrogation by King Humanitie is characterised by long pentameter lines, but the pace is accelerated by John completing the King's rhyming couplets (lines 2442–7):

> REX: **Schaw** me thy **name**, gude **man**, I **the** com**mand**.
> JOHNE: Marie, **John** the **Com**mon-**weill** of **fair** Scot**land**.
> REX: The **Com**mon-**weill** hes **bene** a**mang** his **fais**!
> JOHNE: Ye, **Sir**, that **gars** the **Com**mon-**weill** want **clais**.
> REX: **Quhat** is the **caus** the **Com**mon-**weill** is cru**kit**?
> JOHNE: Be**cause** the **Com**mon-**weill** hes **bene** over**lu**kit!

All in all, Lyndsay in *Ane Satyre of the Thrie Estaitis* combines his technical skill as a poet, of grand and comic verse, with a keen ear for dramatic dialogue. The verse forms flow fluently from one episode to the next, giving a variety and change of pace to the succession of scenes in the play.

Activity
Look at the play and identify a transition point from one episode to another – e.g. an episode featuring the virtuous characters cutting into an episode featuring the vices. Read the lines out loud, before and after the transition, and mark where you might stress a syllable, as in the syllables shown in bold above. Count the number of stressed syllables before and after the transition point. Is there a change in pattern?

Now look at the rhyme schemes before and after the transition point. Are the rhymes couplets (aabb), 4-line stanzas (abab), tail-rhyme (aabccb), or something else? Does the pattern change after the transition point? Does the pace quicken or slow down?

10. TWO KEY SCENES

The full version of *Ane Satyre of the Thrie Estaitis* is such a long, digressive production that a focus on any selected scenes runs the risk distorting it by narrowing its scope. Is it a story of one man's fall and redemption? If so, look at the seduction of Humanitie by Sensualitie (lines 102–553), and his redemption at the hand of Divyne Correctioun (lines 1677–1784). Is it a political play about the revolt of the common man (or woman) against the oppression of the church? If so, then look at the interlude with the Pauper and Pardoner (lines 2087–2300), then skip forward to John the Common-weill's angry intrusion into parliament to accuse the Three Estates (lines 2359–2497). Is it a play about the essential foolishness of human nature? If it is, you might care to focus on the mock baptisms (lines 602–807), in which the vices disguise themselves as virtues, and on Foly's sermon (lines 4272–4673). The baptisms would have had a particular topicality in a play performed a few days after Whit Sunday, since on that day, the seventh Sunday after Easter each year, those who were baptised traditionally wore white robes. In short, the play offers possibilities for different kinds of reading.

For the present purposes, I have chosen two episodes that feature perhaps the two most popular and striking characters in the play, Flatterie and John the Common-weill.

The Entrance of Flatterie (see lines 554–650)

To gauge the impact of Flatterie's entrance, it is probably best to look also at Gude Counsall's opening speech, immediately beforehand (lines 554–601). Contrast the language and imagery used in Gude Counsall's speech with that used by Flatterie as he introduces himself, and then begins to converse with the other vices (lines 602–650). The structure of the episode is as follows:

- Gude Counsall begins with a blessing, directly invoking God's mercy on the audience, whom he addresses as 'gude friends'.

- He tells the audience his mission in life is to offer wise advice to kings and emperors.
- He contrasts his hospitable reception in England and France to his banishment in Scotland, where he has been replaced by 'vicious counsell'.
- Still, he clings to the hope that even now his honour will be restored and that the King will be guided by reason. Meantime he takes a rest.
- Flatterie then enters, crying out for people to 'mak roume'. He shows off his multi-coloured clothes, and promises his news if the crowd will keep quiet.
- He tells the audience that since his last appearance at Christmas, he has been adrift in a storm-tossed boat, wrecked near the isle of May.
- He vividly describes how his fear made him break wind and empty his bowels, making such a smell that even the Devil would not dare approach his buttocks.
- However, he has now escaped and he asks the audience to recognise him.
- He then calls on his fellow vices, calling first on Falset.
- They meet as old friends, and Flatterie asks after Dissait. Falset replies that he left him drinking in the town, but he will arrive 'incontinent'.

In terms of characterisation and staging, the following issues are worth addressing:

- Flatterie is conventionally dressed in multi-coloured clothes ('motley') to symbolise his inconstancy. How do you imagine Gude Counsall would be dressed?
- Look at Gude Counsall's speech. Lyndsay varies its style in the central section, moving from stately five-stress metre, rhyming *abab* to quicker four-stress metre, rhyming *aaabcccb*. The change in metre and rhyme correspond to a shift in topic.

A Satire of the Three Estates

- How do you imagine Gude Counsall would express his emotions at being banished by King Humanitie?
- How do you think Flatterie enters – from the side of the performance area or through the audience itself?
- Flatterie tells the audience that he has been gone since Christmas. Much to the church's official disapproval, holidays were associated with popular celebration and the indulgence of vice.
- One of the most popular books in Europe at the time of Lyndsay's play was called *The Shyp of Folys* ('The Ship of Fools'). Flatterie's detailed story of his shipwreck might allude to this popular theme.
- How do Flatterie and Falset refer to each other? How do they show their affection?
- 'Incontinent' has the possible double meaning of 'soon' and 'drunk'. These two meanings are a result of the conflation of two Old French borrowings into English and Scots – *incontinant* 'straight away', and *incontinent,* 'unrestrained' 'unable to hold water'.

The potential audience reaction can also be considered:

- How do you think the audience would respond to Flatterie's direct questions: 'Quhat say ye, sirs, am I not gay?' and 'Se ye not Flatterie, your awin fule?' In comparison with Gude Counsall, how might the audience feel about Flatterie?
- The characterisation of a severe Gude Counsall and an ingratiating and funny Flatterie might dramatise the dilemma that wise advice is often shunned, while flatterers are popular characters.
- Unlike his fellow vices, Flatterie will eventually escape hanging. Do you think his survival would have met with the audience's approval? Does it weaken Lyndsay's moral 'message'?

John the Common-weill's Complaint (lines 2520–2851)
John Common-weill's complaint is a much longer episode than Flatterie's entrance, and only the opening section of it is considered in detail below. The central pivot of the second half of the play, John's complaint, allows the representatives of the common people, the Pauper and his advocate John, to give a detailed account to the parliament of the Three Estates of the sufferings that ordinary folk have endured at the hands of the temporal and spiritual Estates. The structure of the opening section of this episode is as follows:

- On the advice of Gude Counsall, the temporal Estates, that is, the nobles and the merchants, invite John the Common-weill to speak. He asks to be accompanied by the Pauper, and, again on Gude Counsall's advice, this is permitted.
- John first attacks those Scottish 'traitors' who oppress the common folk, asking how they are supposed to defend the country against English foes if they are not even protected against their own thieves.
- He then attacks 'idle men' of various kinds, from beggars and wandering vagrants to those members of the church who do no work. John shows his learning by comparing them unfavourably with philosophers and religious men and women of the past, who professed poverty, did little work, but lived without luxury, according to their beliefs.
- Next, John attacks corrupt judges who give disproportionately harsh sentences to poor people, while allowing the wealthy and powerful to escape the law.
- Correctioun acknowledges the force of John's complaint and asks the temporal lords to reorganise their lands so that hard-working labourers will profit from them. The lords respond that they are content to do so, if the spiritual authorities do likewise. The spiritual Estate reserves its judgement.

A Satire of the Three Estates

- Correctioun then exerts further pressure, and the temporal lords submit to him. On their repentance, Correctioun pardons them for their earlier sins.
- Correctioun invites John to complain specifically against the spiritual Estate, the churchmen. John at first refuses, for fear of reprisal, but when Correctioun assures him of protection, he launches an attack on the corruption of the church.
- His first complaint is against the death tax by which priests can acquire the property of poor people who suffer bereavement. The Pauper bears witness to the suffering caused by this practice.
- John follows this up with the accusation that those who hold religious office are more interested in receiving taxes than preaching; the Pauper again backs up his accusations.
- Members of the spiritual Estate interrupt John and the Pauper at this point, accusing them of heresy and threatening them with being burned at the stake. A fierce argument ensues, eventually halted by Gude Counsall.
- The Merchant restates the temporal Estates' desire to reform their practices so that hard-working labourers are protected in making a profitable living, so long as they are willing to fight for their king when the occasion arises.
- The spiritual Estate again refuses to mend its ways and is ultimately over-ruled by the majority represented by the lords and the merchants. John acknowledges the promised reforms, but adds that the taxes that the church pays to Rome should also remain in Scotland. Another round of disputation ensues.

As for characterisation in this episode, the following issues can be addressed:

- This is effectively a trial scene, with Divyne Correctioun standing as God's judge on earth. But

who is the accused? John the Common-weill and the Pauper put the Three Estates on trial; the church attempts to re-frame the debate as the trial of two heretics. Divyne Correctioun's sympathies may be with John, and he offers his protection, but the common man still has to stand up to the institutional power of the church.
- Both parties are familiar with legal procedures, as we can see in the recurring phrase 'I tak an instrument'. This term refers to a legal document called a 'notarial instrument' which was brought to the judge's notice as evidence of past legal practices in order to support a case.
- Why did Lyndsay have two representatives of the common people – John the Common-weill and the Pauper? John seems to act more as a legal advocate, an articulate representative of the common folk who displays erudition and knowledge of legal procedures. The Pauper functions more as an example of someone who has been victimised by the spiritual and secular authorities.
- The behaviour of the temporal and spiritual Estates is shown to be quite different, in that the nobles and merchants repent of their former iniquities quite quickly. Spiritualitie, however, clings stubbornly to its power and privileges, and responds to the accusations against it with fury.
- In the heat of an increasingly bitter argument, Gude Counsall attempts to calm things down, acting like the chairman in an ill-tempered meeting who has to keep angry participants to the points of an agreed agenda.

This is a long and involved discussion, and it is interesting to speculate how the common folk in the audience would have responded to it. Fictional trials are still a popular source of drama today, but they usually depend on the victim engaging our sympathy, and the person who is oppressing the victim provoking our intense dislike. There is plenty here to provoke discussion in class. For example, would the 16th century crowd, several hours into the drama by now, have taken to John the Common-weill as their spokesman? Would they have been impressed by his plain-spoken authority, his familiarity with the law, and his courage when faced with the threat of torture and death? Would they have identified with the Pauper's stories, and perhaps shouted out their own examples of similar hardship? Would they have dared to boo the obviously hypocritical representatives of the still-powerful church? Would they have distinguished between these hypocritical representatives and the moral force represented by Divyne Correctioun? How would they have felt about the lords and merchants of the temporal Estates? Would they have forgiven them as easily as Divyne Correctioun does?

As we have seen, Linday's 16th century audiences were obviously mixed, quite literally ranging from paupers to princes, and even taking in a few spies along the way. How would the noblemen and women in the audience have responded to the upstart figure of John the Common-weill? And – crucially – how would the clergymen? We have evidence that in the first performance of the shorter version of the play, James V jumped up afterwards and threatened his bishops with exile to England if they did not change their ways. In the conclusion of the longer version of the play, Diligence (possibly played by Lyndsay) asks forgiveness if the content of the play was 'to sum men odious'. How would the targets of *Ane Satyre* have felt?

11. MODERN VERSIONS AND PRODUCTIONS

Almost five hundred years passed from the last-known performance of *Ane Satyre of the Thrie Estaitis* in Lyndsay's lifetime, and the first revival of the modern age. The play was printed in the early 1600s but not, so far as we know, performed. And so, very occasional performances of several excerpts notwithstanding, it languished until 1948, when, as noted earlier, the organisers of the then young Edinburgh International Festival wished to stage a play with a Scottish flavour. A collaboration between theatre director Tyrone Guthrie and dramatist Robert Kemp resulted in an edited version of *Ane Satyre of the Thrie Estaitis* being presented, somewhat ironically, at the Assembly Hall of the Church of Scotland. The stage in the Assembly Hall allowed the audience to be seated on three sides of the performance area, thus reconstituting something of the atmosphere of the 16th century performances. The success of this revival was such that the play has been staged a number of times, in Edinburgh and beyond. The most recent large-scale productions of Kemp's acting text, directed by Tom Fleming between 1984 and 1991, toured as far afield as Poland. An audio recording of excerpts of this version was made in 1984.

Matthew McDiarmid's edition of Kemp's acting script, first published in 1967, is still sometimes used as a teaching text. The main differences between this version and the text printed by Charteris are:

- the cutting of the Sowtar's divorce from his wife, as performed by the Pardoner (lines 2087–2186). Even to modern tastes this episode tends to be regarded as too obscene to be staged.
- the cutting of the details of the Acts of Parliament (lines 3823–3981), which were considered to be too specific to the 16th century to hold the interest of a modern audience
- the conflation of various characters thought to be similar, the main example of which is Flatterie,

the Pardoner and Foly. One outcome of this is that Flatterie seems to appear in Kemp's version in several extra guises; Lyndsay might well have wished to keep these characters apart.

Longer and shorter versions of the play have since been performed in various venues: 1969 saw an ambitious attempt to stage a fuller version of the play in Glasgow University's Bute Hall; in 1995 a much shorter version was performed and filmed in the same setting by an amateur company, as part of the entertainment laid on for an international conference of scholars of English. The 1990s also saw Greyfriar's Kirkyard in Edinburgh become the scene of a 25-minute extract filmed for the Open University, with John the Common-weill first becoming 'Jane'.

In 1998 a translation in slightly archaic English was published by Nigel Mace. He again cut down the Charteris version of the play, but in a different way from Robert Kemp. Mace omits the Sowtar's divorce and the enumeration of the Acts of Parliament, but also cuts out the episodes featuring Foly at the end of the play. He conflates the roles of Covetice and Common Thift, and plays down the more misogynistic references to the female anatomy. His version is worth seeking out, if only for the lively introduction; his version has not, so far as I know, been performed yet. The casting allows for 'John' the Common-weill to become 'Jane'.

Perhaps the most notable of recent adaptations and performances, in 2000, returned the play to its origins on Castle Hill in Cupar. The poet, playwright and novelist Alan Spence's 'millennium version' of *The 3 Estaites* updates the language to modern Scots and the references to present-day Scotland – for instance, the comedian Billy Connolly is referred to as a fool, the modern counterpart of Lyndsay's Gilly-moubrand or Cacaphatie (lines 4643–4647). In Spence's version, John the Common-weill again becomes 'Jane the Common-weil', and Lyndsay's version is slimmed down into a Proclamation plus 37 scenes. The Sowtar's divorce and the Acts of Parliament are still deemed unplayable, but Foly is restored as a character alongside Flatterie, and his sermon again foreshadows the close of the play.

The existence of various modern versions and adaptations underscores the fact that each new edition of the play involves an interpretation of it. After nearly half a millennium of neglect, the play enjoyed a spectacular second life in the second half of the 20th century. The story of *Ane Satyre of the Thrie Estaitis* looks set to continue.

Activity
Compare the following extract from Lyall's critical edition of the play (lines 3687–98), based on Charteris' printed version, with later editions and adaptations by (a) Kemp/McDiarmid, (b) Mace and (c) Spence shown on the next page. Then take another speech from the play and update it in a manner of your own choosing.

PRIORES: I gif my freinds my malisoun
   That me compellit to be ane nun,
      And wald nocht let me marie.
   It was my freindis greadines
   That gart me be ane Priores –
      Now hartlie them I warie.
   Howbeit that nunnis sing nichts and dayis,
   Thair hart waitis nocht quhat thair mouth sayis:
      The suith I yow declair
   Makand yow intimatioun
   To Christis congregatioun
      Nunnis ar nocht necessair.

A Satire of the Three Estates

(a) PRIORESS: I give my friends my malisoun
   That me compellt to be a nun,
         And wald nocht let me marry!
   It was my friendis greediness
   That gart me be a Prioress.
         Now heartly I them wary!
   Howbeit that Nuns sings nichts and days
   Their heart wots nocht what their mouth says,
         The sooth I you declare;
   Makand you intimatioun,
   To Christis congregatioun
         Nuns are nocht necessare.

(b) PRIORESS; Those friends of mine I lay a curse on,
   That me compelled to be a nun,
         And would not let me marry:
   It was my own friends' greediness
   That made me be a Prioress –
         May now the Fiend them harry!
   Although nuns sing both night and day
   Their hearts know not what their mouths say,
         The truth I you declare;
   Making you intimation,
   That in Christ's congregation
         Nuns are not needed there.

(c) PRIORESS: My curses upon every one
   That did compel me be a nun,
   And wouldnae let me marry.
   It was my family's greediness
   That made me be a Prioress
   So they should pay nae dowry.
   Howbeit that nuns sing nicht and day,
   Their hearts feel nocht what their mooths say,
   And so the truth it runs.
   Now here I gie ye intimation
   Tae all within Christ's congregation –
   There is nae need for nuns.

12. THE INFLUENCE OF *ANE SATYRE OF THE THRIE ESTAITIS*

Given that the play lay dormant for well nigh five hundred years, before being successfully revived and serially adapted, its influence on subsequent drama might be considered to be slight. This may indeed be true; however, there are some hints of influence that might fruitfully be pursued.

The Reformation, which the religious conflict described in the play anticipates, was eventually to suppress much theatrical activity in Scotland. While the theatre blossomed under royal patronage in Elizabethan and Jacobean England, the increasingly puritanical force of the Protestant church in Scotland stifled theatrical development in Scotland until the 18th century, by which time popular taste did not favour medieval revivals. *Ane Satyre of the Thrie Estaitis* therefore remained the first, greatest and least performed Scottish play until midway through the 20th century, when its success at the Edinburgh International Festival gave some Scottish dramatists a new-found confidence and a sense of recovered history. The characteristics of the play that seem to have appealed to later dramatists include its vigorous and unapologetic use of Scots; the unconventional places where it was staged, whether in the open air, a palace banqueting hall, or indeed in the Church of Scotland Assembly Hall; the way it oscillates from farce to high ceremony, using music and song along the way to punctuate its pageantry; and its mixture of crowd-pleasing comedy and sharp-toothed contemporary political and moral satire.

Similar ingredients can be found in several Scottish plays that have been dramatic milestones over the past fifty years. In the 1970s, John McGrath's play *The Cheviot, The Stag and the Black, Black Oil,* also toured unconventional sites such as village halls, and re-imagined theatrical performance as a ceilidh. McGrath combined a comedy full of stereotypical figures with a satirical view of Scottish history in which the common man and woman had been victimised, generation upon generation, by institutions that gave legitimacy to greedy landowners and speculators. Performed in English with some Gaelic by the openly propagandist 7:84 theatre company, this was popular theatre as a social crusade.

The influence of Guthrie's 1948 production of a Scottish medieval morality play can be traced in the Scottish director and playwright Bill Bryden's re-imagining of the York and Wakefield Mystery Plays in the late 1970s, a National Theatre production, again performed at the Edinburgh Festival. This directorial experience no doubt had an impact on Bryden's production of his own play, *The Ship,* a nostalgic celebration of the kind of hard-working common man lauded by John the Common-weill. This spectacle was performed in the unconventional space of the Harland and Wolff shipyard in Govan in 1980. With dialogue in a rich, urban Scots, *The Ship*, too, ended with a ceilidh.

It is perhaps too easy to be glib about the impact of *Ane Satyre of the Thrie Estaitis* on contemporary playwrights. In the 1980s, at one of a series of gatherings of Scottish dramatists, few playwrights admitted to having seen the play or having been directly influenced by it. Liz Lochhead even characterised its language as 'foustie' – musty and old-fashioned. A generation or so after its initial revival, perhaps the play had become an establishment icon to be challenged anew. Indeed, Liz Lochhead's *Mary Queen of Scots Got her Head Chopped Off* (1987) imagines the stormy period just after Lyndsay's time as an elaborate playground game featuring two rival queens, locked in political and religious conflict. As well as its moral and religious themes, Lochhead's play shares with *Ane Satyre* the sudden shifts from farce to tragedy. For Lochhead, the roots of modern sectarianism can be traced back in time to the religious debates that embroiled France, Scotland and England for so long and with such violent results.

More recently, the Iraq conflict acted as the violent backdrop to Gregory Burke's celebrated *Black Watch* (2006). Although this play focuses on the soldiers of a Scottish regiment, the play can be seen as part of the tradition, established by *Ane Satyre,* of celebrating, through tragedy and humour, the victimised but resilient common man's struggle against powerful, self-interested institutions, in this case the politicians and the army. Again, the initial productions were 'on site', the first taking place in a Drill Hall in Forest Hill, Edinburgh in 2006.

Echoes of *Ane Satyre of the Thrie Estaitis,* then, can be heard in much modern Scottish drama, even when the playwrights are ambivalent about its influence on them. However, perhaps the most suggestive influence of Lyndsay's drama, is one of the earliest. Although it was not performed in 16th century England, *Ane Satyre of the Thrie Estaitis* was printed in London in 1604, just after the accession of James V's grandson, James VI of Scotland, to the throne of England. James VI and I found himself in London at the height of a theatrical culture of which he became the principal patron. The troupe run by the most celebrated playwright of the day, William Shakespeare, was renamed 'the King's Men', and around 1605–6, Shakespeare wrote the tragedy of *Macbeth,* to honour the new King's ancestral lineage, and to indulge his interest in witchcraft. We know that Shakespeare read accounts of Scottish history, such as Bellenden's Scots translation of Hector Boece's Latin *Chronicles of Scotland,* when researching the play.

Between 1603 and 1606, at much the same time as he wrote *Macbeth,* Shakespeare wrote *King Lear,* perhaps his most powerful tragedy. *King Lear* tells the story of a mythical British king who mistakes flattery for true love. Lear rejects the good counsel of his faithful servant, Kent, and ignores home truths voiced by a Fool. True love in the play is represented by his daughter, Cordelia, who combines the virtues of chastity and verity. Flattery is present in her two sisters, Regan and Goneril, who also embody the vices of sensuality, danger and deceit. Flattery and deceit are the ruling passions of the main villain of the play, Edmund, who causes his father's eyes to be put out. What hope for the future there is in this bleak play lies not in divine correction but in Lear's belated, mad self-realisation, and in the moral progress of the enigmatic character of Edgar. Edgar, Edmund's half-brother, an inexperienced young man, has to take on the guises of a Pauper and even a witless Fool before emerging as the hope of the next generation.

In short, a dark morality play of virtue and vice, with many similar ingredients to *Ane Satyre of the Thrie Estaitis,* albeit often in disguise, runs through *King Lear.* We know that Shakespeare had many other sources for this play, most notably Raphael Holinshed's *The Chronicles of England, Scotlande, and Irelande* (1587), and we know that morality play characters were the stock-in-trade of much of the English dramatic tradition. But it would be surprising if the king's favourite playwright had neglected to read a play printed just as he was composing his own work, the first London publication of a play specifically devised for his patron's grandfather.

13. CONCLUSION

But let us in conclusion return briefly to where we started, on Castle Hill in Cupar, a good few hours later, on that warm summer's evening of 1552. By now the play is over, the grass on the hill is trampled down by the weight of bodies, and the odours of ale, sweat and urine mingle with the usual smells of hay and cattle, drifting across town on the breeze from the nearby meadows. It has been a remarkable day. The dissipating crowds are still laughing, recalling lines of dialogue, re-enacting favourite moments, arguing theological points, expressing shock, disgust, delight and anger in equal amounts. Some were outraged, some were bored, and now a young mother carries home a sleeping child. The exhausted players are slowly packing up their props and costumes, and chatting to wide-eyed admirers. The ale-house beckons. Scottish theatre has begun.

14. FURTHER READING

Editions
All of the editions of the play mentioned below have rather different introductions and commentaries. All are worth reading to get a variety of perspectives on the play.

Hamer, Douglas, ed. *The Works of Sir David Lyndsay of the Mount 1490–1555,* Vols I–IV, Edinburgh and London: Scottish Text Society and William Blackwood & Sons, 1931. For the serious student of the plays, this is still the fullest edition, though most will only be able to consult it in a library. Volume II contains three versions of the play: the notes taken at the Linlithgow performance of 1540, the Bannatyne manuscript edition, and the Charteris printed edition. Copious notes are given in the later volumes.

Happé, Peter, ed. *Four Morality Plays,* Harmondsworth: Penguin, 1979. Includes a full version of *Ane Satyre* based on Charteris, alongside three English Morality Plays, *The Castle of Perseverance, Magnyfycence* and *King Johan.*

Jack, Ronald D.S and P.A.T. Rozendaal, *The Mercat Anthology of Early Scottish Literature, 1375–1707,* Edinburgh: Mercat Press, 1997. This anthology prints only the first act of *Ane Satyre of the Thrie Estaitis;* in compensation, however, there is the opportunity to read this extended extract of the play in the context of Scottish literature of the period immediately preceding and succeeding it.

Lyall, Roderick, ed. *The Thrie Estaitis, Sir David Lyndsay* Edinburgh: Canongate, 1989. Part of the 'Canongate Classics' series, this is the most accessible modern critical edition, now available as a digital reprint, and it has been used as the basis for this Scotnote. All line numbers refer to this edition.

Mace, Nigel, trans. *Sir David Lyndsay: The Three Estates: A Pleasant Satire in Commendation of Virtue and in Vituperation of Vice* Aldershot: Ashbrook, 1998. A translation into a slightly archaic English by someone whose passion for and knowledge of the play shines through his introduction.

McDiarmid, Matthew, ed. *A Satire of the Three Estates by Sir David Lyndsay* London: Heinemann, 1967. A version by Matthew McDiarmid from the shortened acting text made by Robert Kemp for Tyrone Guthrie's production at the Edinburgh Festival 1948. Lyndsay's spellings are slightly modernised, making this more accessible to beginners than the Lyall edition.

Spence, Alan, trans. *David Lyndsay's The 3 Estaites: The Millennium Version* Edinburgh: Edinburgh University Press, 2002. A loose, shortened adaptation into lively modern Scots, with an equally lively introduction by Angus Calder.

Walker, Greg, ed. *Medieval Drama: An Anthology* Oxford: Blackwell, 2000. This scholarly edition includes the description of the 1540 interlude and the complete text of the 1552 play. Like Happé's anthology, it offers the opportunity to see how the play relates to other forms of drama, such as miracle and morality plays.

Secondary Reading

Barron, Charles, *Drama: The 3 Estaites Learning and Teaching Guide [Higher]* Glasgow: Learning and Teaching Scotland, 2003. (This teaching guide is to Alan Spence's 'Millennium Version' of the play.)

Carpenter, Sarah, 'Early Scottish Drama' in *The History of Scottish Literature, Vol 1: Origins to 1660,* Ronald D. Jack (ed.) Aberdeen: Aberdeen University Press, 1988, pp. 199–211

Edington, Carol, *Court and Culture in Renaissance Scotland: Sir David Lyndsay of the Mount* Amherst: University of Massachusetts Press, 1994

Findlay, Bill, 'Beginnings to 1700' in *A History of Scottish Theatre,* Bill Findlay (ed.) Edinburgh: Edinburgh University Press, 1998, pp. 1–79

Findlay, Bill, 'Theatre and Drama' in *Scottish Life and Society: A Compendium of Scottish Ethnology, Volume 10: Oral Literature and Performance Culture,* John Beech, Owen Hand, Fiona MacDonald, Mark A. Mulhern and Jeremy Weston McGavin (eds.) Edinburgh: Birlinn, 2007, pp. 531–555

Tydeman, William, 'Agreable to hys pageaunt': some thoughts on medieval acting' in *Acting Medieval Plays* by Peter Meredith, William Tydeman and Keith Ramsay, Lincoln: Honywood Press, Lincoln Cathedral Library, 1985, pp. 27–46

Williams, Janet Hadley, (ed.) *Sir David Lyndsay: Selected Poems* Glasgow: Association for Scottish Literary Studies, 2000

Other Resources

A DVD of *The Gathering 1970–2005,* a series of discussions featuring contemporary Scottish playwrights, is available from the Scottish Society of Playwrights: www.scottishsocietyofplaywrights.co.uk

The Life and Times of Sir David Lyndsay is a network of academics, teachers, students, writers, directors and performers who collaborate in the sharing of research news, queries, and general information concerning pre-Reformation literature in general, and the works of Sir David Lyndsay in particular. Those interested in joining the group are invited to contact Professor Greg Walker at greg.walker@ed.ac.uk

15. TIMELINE

This brief chronology is offered as a guide to the timeline activities suggested in the Scotnote. It may naturally be supplemented with other events, but it is here intended to put Lyndsay's life and work into a general political and social context. Events specifically to do with Lyndsay or his work are italicised.

- c.1486: *Lyndsay is born, eldest son of a small landholder.*
- 1488: James III dies. James IV becomes King of Scotland.
- 1503: James IV marries Margaret Tudor, daughter of Henry VII of England.
- 1508: *'David Lyndesay' is recorded as entering the Scottish court as a groom; possibly he is the future poet and playwright.*
- 1509: Henry VIII, Margaret Tudor's brother, becomes King of England.
- 1511: *A payment is recorded, to David Lyndsay, for a costume worn in a play performed before James IV and Margaret Tudor.*
- 1512: The future James V is born; *Lyndsay is appointed his companion.*
- 1513: James IV dies at the Battle of Flodden, leaving the infant James V as King of Scots. *Lyndsay continues to be his companion.*
- 1517: In Germany, Martin Luther publishes his 'ninety-five theses', questioning the authority of the Catholic Church, and inspiring the Reformation in Europe.
- Early 1520s: *Lyndsay marries Janet Douglas, the King's seamstress.*
- 1524: James V is declared fit to rule under the guardianship of Archibald Douglas, Earl of Angus. *Lyndsay ceases to be the King's companion but remains at court.*
- c.1526: *Lyndsay writes his poem, 'The Dreme'.*

A Satire of the Three Estates

- 1528: James V begins to rule in his own right. *Lyndsay is reinstated as the king's close companion.*
- c. 1530: *Lyndsay becomes a herald at the Scottish court. He writes 'A Complaynt' and 'The Testament of the Papyngo' and begins diplomatic travel, particularly to France, sometimes by way of England.*
- 1534: Henry VIII becomes head of the Church of England.
- 1537: James V marries Madeleine, daughter of Francis I of France, who dies shortly afterwards. *Lyndsay is involved in the marriage negotiations, and writes a 'Flyting' with the king.*
- 1538: James V marries Mary of Guise, daughter of a powerful French Catholic family. *Lyndsay organises the formal celebrations.*
- 1542: *In Linlithgow Palace, on Twelfth Night, in January, an 'interlude' that is a short, early version of* Ane Satyre of the Thrie Estaitis *is performed before James V and Mary of Guise. A report is sent to Henry VIII.* Later that year, James V is wounded at the battle of Solway Moss, fighting the English army. He dies shortly after the birth of his daughter, Mary, Queen of Scots. *Lyndsay organises James V's funeral.* James Hamilton, 2nd Earl of Arran, takes control of Scotland while Mary is a child.
- 1544: The 'rough wooing' begins. The infant Mary is betrothed to Prince Edward of England by the Treaty of Greenwich (1543) but the Scottish parliament revokes this treaty, sparking a long series of violent conflicts between England and Scotland.
- 1546: *Lyndsay negotiates the release of hostages taken at St Andrews Castle by the Protestant murderers of Cardinal Beaton. He later writes the satirical poem, 'The Tragedie of the Cardinall'.*
- 1547: Mary, Queen of Scots, is sent to France, where she grows up. Henry VIII dies, succeeded by Elizabeth I.

- 1548: *Lyndsay travels to Protestant Denmark on a diplomatic mission. He later writes his last major poem, 'Ane Dialog...of the Miserabyll Estait of the Warld.'*
- 1552: *After the Cupar Banns are announced, the full version of* Ane Satyre of the Thrie Estaitis *is performed in Cupar, Fife, on June 7th.*
- 1554: James Hamilton relinquishes control of Scotland to Mary of Guise, who rules as Queen Regent. *In August, a revised version of* Ane Satyre of the Thrie Estaitis *is performed again, in Edinburgh, before the Queen Regent, Mary of Guise.*
- 1555: *Lyndsay's death is recorded in a charter of 13th March.*
- 1560: The Presbyterian Church in Scotland is established under the leadership of John Knox. Mary of Guise dies.
- 1561: Mary, Queen of Scots, returns to Scotland to begin ruling in person. She is opposed by the Scottish Protestants.
- 1566: The future James VI of Scotland and I of England is born.
- 1568: Mary abdicates and flees to England, putting herself under the protection of Elizabeth I. James VI becomes King of Scots at the age of two. He is raised as a Protestant. *George Bannatyne, an Edinburgh merchant, leaves the capital for the country to escape a bout of the plague. He passes the time compiling a manuscript of literary works. One of the texts he includes is a version of* Ane Satyre of the Thrie Estaitis.
- 1586: Mary, Queen of Scots, is executed in England.
- 1602: *Robert Charteris publishes the full version of* Ane Satyre of the Thrie Estaitis *in Edinburgh.*
- 1603: On Elizabeth I's death, James VI of Scotland inherits the English throne. The Scottish court moves to London.

- 1604: *Robert Charteris publishes a slightly altered reprint of* Ane Satyre of the Thrie Estaitis *in London.*
- 1948: *At the Edinburgh International Festival, Tyrone Guthrie's acclaimed production of Robert Kemp's shortened version of* Ane Satyre of the Thrie Estaitis *begins the play's modern performance history.*

16. ANSWERS TO VOCABULARY ACTIVITY

1. als: *as also*
2. althocht: *although*
3. awin: *own*
4. ay: *ever/always*
5. baith: *both*
6. be: *be, by*
7. beir: *carry*
8. but: *but/without*
9. eine: *eyes*
10. fra: *from*
11. gang: *go*
12. gif, give: *if*
13. haif: *have*
14. intill: *into*
15. lufe: *love*
16. luik: *look*
17. maist: *most*
18. na: *no/nor/than*
19. nane: *none*
20. nocht: *not*
21. nor: *than*
22. or: *before*
23. quha: *who*
24. quhair: *where*
25. quhen: *when*
26. quhilk: *which*
27. quhill: *until*
28. sen: *since*
29. sic/sik: *such*
30. sould: *should*
31. sune: *soon*
32. syne: *then*
33. thir: *these*
34. till: *to*
35. yit: *yet*